BRISTOL

Beyond the Bridge

'BEYOND THE BRIDGE a Second City Grows'

W. Goldwin – Master of the Grammar School, Bristol 1712

With best wishes

Michael Manson

MICHAEL MANSON

past & present
press

Published by Past & Present Press,
92 Sefton Park Road, St Andrews, Bristol BS7 9AL
Bristol: Beyond the Bridge
ISBN 0-9532082-2-2
First published in 1988 by Redcliffe Press Ltd
This revised edition published 2000 by Past & Present Press

For Hannah and Matthew Manson

Past & Present Press welcomes manuscripts for consideration for
publication. Do not, however, send irreplaceable material. All
material is submitted and received entirely at the sender's risk.

Design and layout Gillian Marles

CONTENTS

FOREWORD

It's an instructive experience to watch a city evolve and to realise that some of what I wrote thirteen years ago is now itself history. Although I have made a number of amendments to this edition of *Bristol Beyond the Bridge*, the main body of text, however, remains substantially the same as before. My heartfelt thanks to: Gillian Marles for the design and typography; Emily Wade for proof reading; John Sansom of Redcliffe Press who started the ball rolling, and Maggie, Hannah and Matthew who, in the best possible way, bring me back to the present.

Michael Manson, Bristol 2000

From my bedroom window in Redcliffe Parade, I had a spectacular view looking down onto Bristol's Floating Harbour. It was a vista of endless fascination; Redcliffe Bridge in the foreground, the warehouses of Redcliffe Back and Welsh Back to the right and left and in the far distance a glimpse of Bristol Bridge. I relied on St Nicholas' church clock for the time and, with the aid of a telescope, could even read its unique second hand.

After a while, something struck me about this view – the difference between Bristol north and south of the water. The Bristol that I could see to the north of the float was grandly prosperous. Whilst to the south, Redcliffe Back with its hulking empty warehouses was a derelict wasteland. I knew much of the centre of Bristol had been devastated during the Second World War, and even in the 1970s the city still bore the scars, but this contrast started me thinking. I wondered, had there always been such an obvious divide between north and south of the Avon? And why? It was from these thoughts that *Bristol Beyond the Bridge* grew.

Michael Manson, Bristol 1987

ACKNOWLEDGEMENTS

Many people have assisted in various ways in the writing of *Bristol Beyond the Bridge*. For help along the way I am grateful to Chris Challis, Marion Dyer, Trevor Fry, Mike Hallet of DRG, the staff of Bristol Central Reference Library, Sheena Stoddard, Mike Ponsford and Andy King of the City of Bristol Museum and Art Gallery, and Sarah Barnes and John Sansom of Redcliffe Press. Also a tip of the hat to the Redcliffe Paraders who were there at the beginning: Dennis, Digby, Fiona, Fred, Hilary, Karen, Liz, Lucy, Mick, Nick, Nancy and Rosie. And finally thanks to Maggie Moss without whose encouragement and faith the book would never have been completed.

5

M.A.S. delin.

THE OLD BRISTOL BRIDGE.

Bristol Bridge, built 1247. Despite its narrowness, its potential for trade was quickly realised and buildings soon sprang up on both sides of the roadway.

INTRODUCTION

Crossing Bristol Bridge after a pleasant stroll along Corn Street and through St Nicholas Market one enters a bleak area of offices and warehouses. Today it is difficult to believe that Redcliffe, Temple and Thomas Streets were once amongst the liveliest thoroughfares in Bristol. From the present surroundings there is little indication that an important community thrived in this area for over 800 years.

But if one takes the time to look there are signs of a greater past than is immediately apparent. Continue walking down Victoria Street and the building that grabs attention is Temple Church with its ornate leaning tower. Though now sadly gutted, it still reflects the prosperity of its builders. The name Temple is a reminder that this area was once governed by the Knights Templar, the fierce crusading order whose history dates back to 1118. Look around further and many other names give clues to the past; Portwall Lane runs alongside the former site of the invincible thirteenth century city wall, while the name Temple Gate speaks for itself. Nearby, sitting sadly on the edge of a car park is Chatterton's House, the birthplace of the marvellous boy poet who died so young. Across the road, hidden by a hotel, stand the remains of a truncated glass cone representative of one of the area's staple industries. And then, of course, there is the beautiful St Mary Redcliffe Church. 'In all respects the finest parochial church in all England' as Queen Elizabeth I so rightly described it. This magnificent church, the size of a small cathedral, gives an idea of the wealth of Redcliffe's inhabitants during the Middle Ages. Up until the twentieth century much of Bristol's prosperity came from its trade through the docks. Although the docks are now quiet, the massive warehouses and mills (now mostly turned into housing) along Redcliffe Back are reminders of the scale of trade handled by the port in the nineteenth century.

South Bristol, in an indefinable way has always had its own distinct identity. Like many other cities divided by a river – the north and south of the Thames at London or the left and the right banks of the Seine at Paris – the transpontine area has a character all its own. The southern perspective is a side of Bristol's history that has largely been ignored. Yet, of course, no parish is an island, and although divided by a river the Southern Parishes are in many matters inseparable from the remainder of Bristol. *Bristol Beyond the Bridge* could be described as a personal history of Bristol told from the steps of St Mary Redcliffe.

So, *Bristol Beyond the Bridge* tells the story of the three original southern parishes of Bristol – Redcliffe, Temple and St Thomas. Geographically it covers roughly the area enclosed in the loop of the Floating Harbour southwards to The Cut.

Although this book makes no attempt to be a definitive record it will, I hope, give a feel of the times and a glimpse of the characters that have shaped this neglected area of Bristol.

ONE

THE EARLY DAYS

One thousand years ago the area that we now know as Redcliffe was little more than a swampy uninviting patch of land. Nobody lived there; it was inhabited only by grazing animals and wildfowl. Even so, there were two tracks, raised on a wattle causeway in the most sodden places, that led away from a timber bridge that crossed the Avon. One of these tracks went along the wooded river valley to Keynsham, the other, disappearing over a low red cliff, led to the Somerset village of Bedminster.

The early settlement of Redcliffe, named after this reddish sandstone cliff first grew after the Norman conquest. A ribbon of wooden and wattle and daub dwellings gradually appeared alongside the two trackways. Indeed, in early charters this string of houses was merely called Radeclivestret (Redcliffe Street).

But apart from its track side position what was it that encouraged settlement in such a damp, uninviting and defenceless place? The answer can be found in the quay that we now call Redcliffe Back. Here, through the natural flow of the river there was a deep waterfrontage. In time, the fact that ships from as far afield as Ireland, France and even Iceland could moor here was the key to Redcliffe's development.

It is crucial when looking at the early history of Redcliffe to understand that it existed not merely as a suburb of Bristol but as a distinct community in its own right. The reason for this division lay not only in the divide created by the River Avon but also in the fact that Bristol and Redcliffe lay in different administrative areas. To the south of the Avon, Redcliffe on its soggy river flood plane, was in the manor of Bedminster, while to the north of the river Bristol lay in Gloucestershire. Consequently, despite their proximity both areas grew up and were governed independently. It was an independence that over the years was to cause problems between two such youthful and vigorous communities.

Apart from administration it would be ridiculous to deny that Redcliffe and Bristol had affinities. Geographically, socially and economically there was an evident closeness between them. Like reflections in the river dividing them, events in one community were mirrored in the other.

The Redcliffe land was gradually divided between owners. The feudal system was such that the King, who owned all the land in the country, would parcel out his property to tenants as gifts in return for certain services such as the loan of money or manpower. Once they were given property, tenants still had no absolute right to this land and, as we shall shortly see, if they failed in their duties were liable to forfeiture.

In 1145 the eastern part of Redcliffe was granted to the heroic group, the Knights Templar. This eastern strip came to be known as Temple Fee and was soon established as the Templars' administrative centre in the West Country. And so Temple Fee with its own market, its settlement of weavers and its peculiar round chapel was soon also a community in its own right.

In the early Norman period Redcliffe, as part of the manor of Bedminster, was under the charge of Robert, Earl of Gloucester, an illegitimate son of Henry I and potential heir to the throne. Robert of Gloucester owned vast tracts of land in both England and France and through his wide ranging connections he did much to promote Redcliffe's development.

Alongside Robert of Gloucester another powerful local figure of the period was Robert Fitz Harding (died 1171). Fitz Harding held the post of King's Reeve – the official royal representative in Bristol. A perceptive businessman, he invested much of his not insubstantial income in the purchase of land and estates. To this end, some time in the 1140s, Fitz Harding bought the manor of Bedminster, which of course included Redcliffe, from the Earl of Gloucester. And in the next few years, thanks largely to the troubles of King Stephen's reign (1135-1154) Fitz Harding's good fortunes were to take an even greater, and unforeseen, turn for the better.

With Henry I's daughter, Matilda, vying with Stephen for the throne, Stephen's reign collapsed into a prolonged period of baronial anarchy. Redcliffe and Bristol, like much of the West Country, offered allegiance to Matilda. Her son, Henry, even spent four years of his childhood in Bristol. When Stephen died it was this Henry who, unopposed, took over the throne.

After the insecurity of Stephen's reign, Henry II's wise and lively rule brought with it a new direction for Redcliffe's economy. For when Henry II came to the throne he inherited a vast empire, the Angevin Empire, that stretched from the Scottish borders down to the Pyrenees. Indeed, the interests of Henry and his French wife, Eleanor of Aquitaine, lay as much with France as they did with England, so much so that of the thirty-four years of his reign Henry spent twenty-one of these abroad. Nevertheless such strong links with Anjou and Aquitaine could only be of benefit to local trade.

Henry was eager to reward those who had been faithful to his mother Matilda. Thus Robert Fitz Harding, who already owned Redcliffe, was awarded the valuable fiefdom of the Berkeley estates which centred on the Severn Valley in Gloucestershire. This grant of both Berkeley land and title laid the foundations for a remarkable dynasty that would rule over Redcliffe for the next two hundred years.

However, there was one problem. The previous baron of the estates, Roger De Berkeley, who had sided with Stephen in the civil war, was meanwhile banished to a dark and dank castle in the shadow of the Cotswold escarpment at Dursley. Needless to say Roger was not pleased to look across the wide Severn Valley and see land that had once been his in the hands of another man. So 'vexed and troubled' was Roger that his discontented rumblings had eventually to be quelled by Henry II with a masterstroke of marriage diplomacy. At the command of the King, Robert Fitz Harding's eldest son, Maurice (1117-1189) married Roger De Berkeley's daughter Alice. It was a fruitful union; not only was the rift between the two families healed, but Alice also bore six sons and a daughter.[1]

Even with his new clutch of land in the Severn Valley, Redcliffe was still Robert Fitz Harding's most valuable asset. If he and the people of Redcliffe were to benefit fully from the new expanded trading connections with France and also Ireland (even in those days there is mention of Bristol's penchant for the trading of slaves, especially young girls) a charter was needed giving freedom from tolls in other areas. Bristol had had such a dispensation since 1155. So some time between 1164 and 1170 Fitz Harding duly sought, and was awarded by Henry II, a charter which granted freedom of customs throughout the land to the men who dwell in the 'marsh near the bridge of Bristol.'[2]

An indication of any community's standing and wealth was given by its ecclesiastical buildings. In a society where everyday life was dominated by the church, a fundamental requirement of even the smallest hamlet was a place of worship. As the settlement of Redcliffe grew, so we find reference to two chapels – those of St Mary and of St Thomas the Martyr. Both were attached to St John's parish church in Bedminster. The humble Norman chapel of St Mary Redcliffe was first mentioned in 1158 when it was given to the cathedral at Salisbury. The foundation of the less famous church of St Thomas came later, probably in the 1170s. Thomas a Becket was martyred on December 29th, 1170; the scandalous manner of his death, murdered by four knights before the altar of Canterbury Cathedral, would account for the dedication.

With time, the Berkeleys moved out of Bristol to their land in the Severn valley and took up residence in Berkeley Castle. They nevertheless continued to look after the needs of the Redclivians. In 1207 Robert Berkeley (1165-1221) granted a supply of fresh clean water to his people by providing a pipeline from the hillside at Knowle to bring spring water down to St Mary Redcliffe. Part of the original conduit still exists and the fountain head can be seen today in the churchyard wall on Redcliffe Hill. From there, there was also a pipeline, the dimensions of a medium sized thumb, that supplied the Hospital of St John in nearby Redcliffe Pit, an institution for the poor also partly supported by the Berkeleys.

So by the beginning of the thirteenth century, Redcliffe with its Berkeley patronage, its charter and its deep waterfrontage looked all set to equal, if not overtake, neighbouring Bristol. Indeed when King John levied aid in 1210 for war in Ireland, both Redcliffe and Bristol contributed the same amount of money[3]. Although Bristol may have been established earlier (the first written mention of Bristol is in 1051 but the fact that the borough had a mint by 1020 shows its importance at a much earlier date) Redcliffe, the late starter, had caught up.

THE GREAT WORKS

It was during the thirteenth century that Redcliffe and Temple Fee united with Bristol to undertake civil engineering works of gargantuan proportions and of such permanence that the city still bears their stamp seven hundred years later.

They were days of boundless energy; the greater part of Bristol had been burnt to the ground in an accident in 1237 yet at the same time the people on both sides of the River Avon were embarking upon costly operations that over the years would involve the building of a new harbour, the construction of a new stone bridge across the river and the extension and strengthening of the town walls.

By 1230 the business transacted in the harbour had grown to such an extent that despite its position up a twisting river and through a gorge that took the wind out of your sails, the port facilities were becoming overcrowded. Bulky cargo ships carrying anything up to 200 tons – 50,000 gallons – of wine from Gascony were sailing up the River Avon and finding berthing awkward. If Bristol was to thrive as a port, albeit a port that at this time relied on imports rather than exports, a new harbour was needed. It was not an easy facility to provide 10 miles from the sea. The plan, however, was this: an enormous trench 2,400 feet long, 120 feet wide and 18 feet deep was to be dug redirecting the River Frome from its curving entry into the Avon just below Bristol Bridge (the Frome ran roughly parallel with today's Baldwin Street) to a more direct route southwards creating new deep water berthing facilities. But to the merchants of Redcliffe and St Thomas there was one catastrophic fault with this bold scheme. It would rob them of their premier waterfrontage. They therefore withheld their support from this grandiose work and were only coaxed into action by a sharply worded writ from the King asserting that the diversion of the Frome was 'for the common good of the whole town' and could not be completed without 'great costs'[4].

Eight years later and at a massive expense of £5,000 the new reach of the Frome, strengthened with stone, was completed and ready to receive the largest ships of the day. Redcliffe and St Thomas' ace card had been trumped; after a brief supremacy their moorings were now eclipsed into second place.

The next great work, the building of a stone bridge across the Avon was of benefit to both communities. Although a wooden bridge had spanned the river for perhaps two hundred years (Bristol is a corruption of the name Brig Stow – fenced place of the Bridge) it was now felt that a new, more stable, even fashionable structure that could cope with increased traffic was needed to link the two sides of the Avon. After all, London's great multi-arched bridge had been erected over fifty years before.

The construction of the bridge in 1247 called for some of the expertise that had already been used in the remodelling of the harbour. The builders' first task was to divert the Avon so that the bridge's foundations could be safely and satisfactorily laid. This was achieved by truncating the loop of the Avon that encompasses Redcliffe, Temple and St Thomas parishes and redirecting it along a ditch. Until 1965 it had been assumed that the full flow of the Avon was able to course along this channel, but excavations in that year have shown that this was unlikely as the Portwall ditch, as it came to be known, would certainly have been inadequate for this purpose.[5] Even so, if only part of the waters of the river were directed it would still have made construction easier especially at low tide.

The completed bridge was a sturdy structure on four arches, the columns of which were so thick that they impeded the flow of the water and, like London Bridge, created a small waterfall. Despite the narrowness of the 19 feet wide bridge its superb potential for trade was soon realised and buildings quickly sprang up on both sides of the roadway. To make the most of the very limited space, this accommodation was partly built on trusses jutting out over the water. The roadway across the bridge took on the aspect of a dark street, its dinginess further increased by the chapel of the Assumption of the Blessed Virgin Mary which was built on an archway straddling the centre of the bridge.

Because ordinances forbade the use of any other material these buildings were built entirely of wood and to lessen the fire risk, roofed with slate. Although the rooms were tiny, the houses were often as many as four storeys high. The ground floor would contain a shop, with perhaps a tiny room behind, a staircase would lead up to a small parlour and kitchen, with two further floors above this and sometimes even an attic. Several houses also had cellars built into the piers of the bridge. Although it was a popular trading site there were some particular disadvantages. It was not unknown for animals being led across the bridge to panic, crash into a shop and run amok. On one occasion a large, powerful ox lumbered through the ground floor of a house and jumped out of its back window, splashing heavily into the water below. Also in times of flood cellars would be awash and there are tales of ships' masts forcing themselves through floorboards with the rising tide.

It was hoped that the new bridge would bring about a spirit of unity. It was mentioned by one optimistic chronicler that 'this year the bridge of Bristow began to be founded and the inhabitants of Redcliffe, Temple and Thomas were incorporated with the town of Bristol…'[7] It was a peace that was not to last for long; squabbles soon broke out over the funding of the third and last 'great work', the improvement of the fortifications.

The inhabitants of Redcliffe, Temple and St Thomas were not happy with the system whereby the murage, a tax collected on goods entering and leaving the town, was pooled. They jealously demanded that the money collected on the southern routes of entry into the town should be put only towards the construction of the southern walls (walls were important not only for defence but also as a means of regulating the collection of tolls). Despite this haggling, the walls to the north of the town were extended and new fortifications enclosing an area of 70 acres (ten more acres than the north) were erected to protect the vulnerable south. To create a hopefully impregnable defensive system the new south wall flanked the north side of the ditch that had originally been dug for the diversion of the Avon.

There were two gateways, Redcliffe and Temple Gate, and an illustration from the seventeenth century indicates that the eight feet thick walls were further strengthened by a series of eight bastions. When Henry VIII's topographer, John Leland, visited Bristol in the 1540s, he was able to report that the Portwall, as it was called, 'is the highest and strongest piece of all the town walls.'[8] He was not wrong; the wall was to stand for many years and indeed was so solidly built that it remained, as we shall see, invincible to all attack until its demolition in the eighteenth century. Interestingly, St Mary Redcliffe, not yet splendid, was stranded outside the fortifications. To direct the defences up Redcliffe Hill would not only have been expensive but also strategically unwise.

THE TEMPLARS

Temple Fee, like Redcliffe, was also administered separately from Bristol. Here the Templars raised their own taxes, held their own courts and ran their own market round their own market cross, the Stallenge, at the north end of Temple Street.

But who were the Templars? Founded in 1118 they first made a name for themselves defending the pilgrim routes to the Holy Land. The twelfth and thirteenth centuries were the era of the crusades, a time that offered a unique opportunity for exotic travel and adventure subsidised by ecclesiastical tithes. The initial impetus for the crusades had arisen in 1098 when Pope Urban II had preached in France that Jerusalem should be rescued from the grip of its Muslim conquerors. From that time on, in a remarkable example of early international cooperation, much money and time was spent transporting armies from north western Europe to the far end of the Mediterranean. It was a long, long way to go and not all those who set out made it. Neither were the intentions of the crusaders always noble – all too often their initial worthy ideals were submerged in an orgy of drunkenness, pillage and rape.

After crossing the choppy seas of the Biscay most crusaders from England would stop off at Oporto. Whilst establishing useful trade links with Portugal this break in the journey also offered a first taste of adventure, as Lisbon, a little further down the coast, was in the hands of the Moors.

It was during the second crusade in 1147 that the men of Bristol made a particularly bad example of themselves. It is recorded that whilst attacking Lisbon their zeal seemed inspired not so much by Christianity as by piracy.[9] The Bristolians were far more interested in the immediate pleasures of looting rather than liberating the Holy Land.

Despite such transgressions, the crusaders and the military orders such as the Templars that backed them were deemed a worthy cause of support; so in 1145 Robert,

Drawn & Engraved by E.Blore.

The Knights of St John made their mark on Temple Fee by building the Church of the Holy Cross.
They did not however account for the softness of the alluvial soil and soon found their church tower
leaning at an alarming angle.

Earl of Gloucester granted the eastern part of Redcliffe to the Knights Templar.

Temple Fee soon became the Templars' headquarters in the south west of England. The order also built itself a small chapel, typical of the Templars in that it was round – the shape reminiscent of the Holy Sepulchre in Jerusalem.

Although these 'Poor Knights of Christ' as the Templars liked to call themselves, started from venerable beginnings – they took the same vows as monks: poverty, chastity and obedience – through their spectacular military achievements they soon became very rich. And in time the Templars, dressed in their distinctive white robes with a red cross emblazoned on the shoulder, became associated more with high-handed arrogance than the humility expected of a quasi-religious order. In England and France they acted as a law unto themselves, recognising only the authority of the Pope. In Temple Fee they certainly paid scant regard to the laws of their neighbours. Not surprisingly such behaviour was to cause their eventual downfall. By 1306, King Philippe of France was anxious to rid his territory of the Templars. He used heresy as a convenient excuse. The Grand Master and several of the knights were burnt at the stake for alleged witchcraft. By 1312, on order of the Pope, the Knights Templar were disbanded. In England, although the Templars were spared the vicious persecution that they received in France, their possessions, which included Temple Fee, were handed over to their rivals, the Hospitaller Knights of St John.

The Knights of St John made their mark on Temple Fee by demolishing the Templars' chapel and on the same spot building their own church. They did not, however, account for the softness of the alluvial ground upon which they were building and soon found that the first stage of their church tower was leaning alarmingly out of skew. Sixty years later, after strengthening the foundations, a second tier was added which also housed a peal of bells. Apocryphal tales abound of how these bells upset the stability of the fine tower even more. On a visit in 1568, the Duke of Norfolk observed the tower's giddy swaying, whilst many years later in the nineteenth century the 'Rural Church Goer' Joseph Leech wrote of a man he met as a boy who used to sit beneath the belfry inserting nuts into the corner stones having them 'incontinently and cleverly cracked as the superstructure swayed with the vibration on the bells.' Leech's comment was that 'the man's *sang-froid* must be great who could enjoy salt and filberts under such circumstances.' [10]

WOOLLEN CLOTH

Apart from its leaning tower, Temple Fee was also famous for its cloth. From the early days of the Templars, Temple Fee had been well known for its settlement of weavers. Even so, it was not until the reign of Edward III that the full potential of the cloth trade was realised and the industry given encouragement to expand. In 1337 the export of raw wool (England's raw wool was acknowledged to be the best in Europe and was eagerly bought by the famous Flemish clothiers) was for a time forbidden. The purpose of this prohibition was twofold: first, to stifle the Italian cloth producers, and second, to encourage the expansion of home production. Additionally, to increase the skilled workforce on the home front, foreign weavers were encouraged to settle and carry out their craft in England. Accordingly Thomas Blanket and a workforce of foreign weavers set up production in Temple Fee in the 1340s. Not surprisingly this foreign, guild breaking workforce was unpopular. Blanket had to seek protection from the King, who also confirmed that it was in order for the continental weavers to be employed.

It ought to be mentioned that the names of Bristol's woollen products can be misleading. There was a striped cloth known as Bristol Cotton that did not contain any cotton whilst the connection between Thomas Blanket and the cloth that bears his name is tenuous. The tale that Blanket was the originator of the cloth is unlikely; in French, *blanchette* means white cloth.

Although cloth workers were to be found on both sides of the river it was in Temple Fee where the majority of them – both indigenous and immigrant – lived. In Temple Fee there was a Tucker Street (tucker being the West Country name for a fuller) and in the new buildings of Temple Church, itself evidence of local prosperity, there was a chapel dedicated to the patron saint of weavers, St Katherine. In fact the manufacture of cloth was so widespread in the parishes of Redcliffe, Temple and Thomas that archaeological investigations into the medieval period invariably uncover related remains. In Cart Lane in 1974 the stumps of the cloth drying racks were uncovered while in 1980 excavations in Redcliffe Street revealed a workshop that had been used by dyers and possibly fullers as well.[11]

So how was the cloth produced? The production of woollen cloth was a relatively complex process involving many operations which would be farmed out to different domestic premises. Much of the combing, carding, cleaning and spinning of the raw fleece would already have been done elsewhere – it was for its weavers that Temple Fee was famous. Once woven, the woollen cloth had to be washed and then tentered, that is hung out to dry and stretched to the correct length on racks. Just south of Temple Church was an area called the Rack Close, equipped with numerous racks set aside for this specific purpose. In 1673 Millerd's map of Bristol showed the Rack Close to still be in existence. Other processes followed: the nap of the cloth had to be raised with the aid of teasels; it was then sheared several times to produce a soft finish, the finest of which was called 'doe skin.' The most popular agent for dying was woad and we find that after wine, woad was the import most mentioned in thirteenth century port records.

But the steady increase in the manufacture of woollen cloth was brought to an abrupt, albeit temporary, halt by the arrival of that curse of medieval and renaissance Europe, the Black Death. Being a port, Bristol was especially vulnerable to such epidemics and with the great mortality of 1349 it suffered badly. Across the country the Black Death killed nine out of ten of its victims. In Bristol local calendars tell how the living were scarcely able to bury the dead.[12] For a while Bristol was a ghost town and on streets that had once been so busy grass began to sprout. 'There died in a manner the whole strength of the town.'

Some of the effects of the Black Death were unexpected. For those who survived, it was an age of opportunity. Remarkably, after the pestilence, the upside-down economy of the country caused the production of wool not to decline but to increase. With fewer people to farm the land, large areas of the countryside were turned over to sheep tracts. The 1350s and 1360s were an outstanding time for Bristol's entrepreneurs with cloth being exported as far afield as Denmark, the Baltic coast, Iceland, France, Spain and other Mediterranean countries.

In short, Edward III's aspirations for a country that produced its own cloth were bearing fruit – though how much his protectionist policies contributed to this is open to speculation. Whatever the reason, England had emerged from the position of Europe's prime wool producer to the more sophisticated role of manufacturer of woollen cloth. In 1348-1349 only 900 cloths had been shipped from Bristol but by 1360 this figure had soared to four and a half thousand.[13] What is more, Bristol was not just a cloth port, it was now the major cloth port of the realm.

TROUBLE WITH THE BERKELEYS

The arrest and imprisonment of a Bristolian in Redcliffe Gaol in 1303 triggered off a series of unexpected and far-reaching events.

As we have already seen, the relationship between Redcliffe and Bristol was frequently strained. The roots of this antagonism lay partly in the differing laws governing the two areas – while Redcliffe was under the control of the Lords of Berkeley, Bristol was ruled by an elected mayor. The Lords of Berkeley held their own court, established a prison and gallows and maintained the right to collect certain taxes. Because of these differences Redcliffe and Bristol looked upon each other with suspicion. Indeed at the beginning of the fourteenth century a state of near civil war existed for a while between the two communities.

Matters came to a head when Richard of Cornwall, a Bristolian, was incarcerated in Redcliffe Street Gaol pending his trial for murder. Some Bristolians may have heard how, forty years before, a fellow burgess was imprisoned by the Berkeleys and promptly, without trial, hanged. Even if they had not heard this tale they were still uncertain that Richard would have a fair trial under the direction of the Berkeleys. So at a meeting hastily summoned by the ringing of the common bell it was resolved to take immediate action to prevent any miscarriage of justice. A large number of people, headed by the Mayor, swarmed across Bristol Bridge and forcibly rescued the prisoner, plundering 500 marks worth (a mark was 13s4d – two thirds of a pound) of Berkeley property as they went.

The Berkeleys were, of course, furious at this outright disregard for their authority. Not only was it a blatant invasion of their rights, it also posed a wider long-term threat to their rule over Redcliffe. Measures had to be taken swiftly to reassert their supremacy. An appeal to the King was therefore lodged, requesting that he appoint a jury to investigate the raid.

Unfortunately no record survives of the outcome of this appeal. Two years later, however, the Bristolians voiced a series of retaliatory petitions, which if they are to be believed show the Berkeleys to be brutal, bullying and corrupt. In comparison, the previous complaints of the Berkeleys fade into triviality.

The tables were turned, it was now the Berkeleys' turn to come under scrutiny. The King appointed two men who, along with the constable of Bristol Castle, were to enquire into the accusation and if they had any difficulty in coming to a decision they were to present their findings to Parliament.

First the Berkeley's court had to be examined; it would appear that not all Redclivians recognised the Berkeleys' jurisdiction and it was claimed that some of these dissenters were dragged from their homes, roughed up and thrown into a pit. In the commotion that followed, several people were trampled and mortally wounded. The impartiality of the Berkeley courts was also in doubt, for it was alleged that 'three lewd thieves and wicked persons', who at Bristol had been imprisoned were taken and retried in Somerton, Somerset and there declared as 'honest men.'[14]

But that was not all; further complaints create a picture of the Berkeley family as the despots of the Severn Vale. In Frampton upon Severn, a Bristolian was so brutally assaulted by Lord Berkeley (died 1321) and his men that shortly afterwards he died. Whilst at Tetbury Fair there was an 'armed rout' of the burgesses of Bristol, many of whom were imprisoned and 'most wickedly…there intreated.' And finally, at Dundry Fair, it was vividly described how Lord Thomas Berkeley, Maurice his son (died 1326) and twenty six henchmen set upon the unfortunate Adam the Cheeseman and 'brake his legs in such a pitiful manner that the marrow came out of his shin bones.'[15]

Not surprisingly, the judgement went against the Berkeleys. They were heavily fined, but more serious, Redcliffe and the rest of the Manor of Bedminster was confiscated.

Yet it was at this time that Robert the Bruce was marauding the northern borders of England and if there was one thing that the King needed as much as money it was good soldiers. It was therefore to the mutual advantage of both parties to come to some agreement over this penalty. Accordingly the 1,000 mark fine was commuted in return for the supply by Lord Berkeley of ten armed horsemen under the command of his son or some other 'fit captayne.' The confiscation of the valuable Manor of Bedminster remained, however. It was a severe blow to the Berkeleys, and they would do their utmost over the following years to secure its return.

For the next few years the Berkeleys made certain they were seen to be faithful allies to the crown. Father and son joined the fighting in the war against Scotland. Thomas himself was captured at Bannockburn but secured release with the payment of a ransom. Nearer to home, Lord Thomas was sent to Bristol to enquire into a revolt over taxation that came to be known as 'the Great Insurrection.' Lord Thomas, not being the paragon of impartiality that the Bristolians had hoped for, was briefly held prisoner but later had the satisfaction of being a major force in the revolt's collapse by blockading the port of Bristol with his boats.

But even so, these displays of allegiance went unrewarded and by the end of Edward II's troubled reign the Berkeleys began to take a very different approach.

For the last few months of his life Edward II was deposed from the throne and held prisoner by his wife, Isabella, and her lover Mortimer. For a while the King was interned in Bristol but in the spring of 1327 he was escorted to Berkeley Castle for 'safe keeping.' Though tales of the manner of Edward's death vary they all have one element in common: extreme sadism. At Berkeley, Edward II was kept 'in a vault up to his knees in water, to which the channels of the castle run.' And it is told how, on a chill autumn night in 1327, the townsfolk of Berkeley were awoken from their sleep by terrible screams from the castle. Many 'prayed to God for the harmless soul which that night was departing in torture.' The next day Edward II was dead. His body, which is reputed to have had no outward signs of violence upon it, was buried some days later at Gloucester Cathedral.

Although the brutal deed occurred at Berkeley Castle, Lord Thomas (died 1361) was keen, not unnaturally, to be disassociated from it. He claimed to be ill at the time, six miles away at Bradley, near Wotton-under-Edge. He was so stricken that he said that he had lost his memory. This plea was subsequently accepted by Parliament and he was absolved of any involvement in the murder. However, Smyth, the Berkeleys' erudite historian, doubts this alibi and notes that Lord Thomas' recovery was swift, for on the day after the killing he was quick to send the news of the regicide to the treacherous Isabella and Mortimer.

Two years later, perhaps prompted by Isabella and Mortimer, the young King Edward III returned the Manor of Bedminster to the Berkeleys. After a twenty five year lapse the Berkeleys were once again in control of their valued Redcliffe.

SOUTHERN PARISHES UNITED WITH BRISTOL

The administrative divide between north and south of what was now England's second largest town made little sense to anybody apart from the Berkeleys and Templars, that is. Despite a charter of 1331,[16] one of many which confirmed that Redcliffe should answer to the jurisdiction of Bristol, the Berkeleys were determined to hold onto their loosely defined privileges.

On top of this Berkeley interference there were other problems. Merchants complained of arduous journeys through deep and dangerous roads to the county courts at Ilminster in Somerset and Gloucester. Such journeys could take two days each way and for those who had property on both sides of the Avon, matters could be even more tiresome.

So, the Mayor and people of Bristol, together with many merchants from the Southern Parishes, petitioned the King to resolve this hindrance to the smooth running of their businesses. With £400 on offer, a beleaguered Edward III, currently suffering financial hardship through war with France, was keen to listen. Though unprecedented, the answer to the merchants' problems was straightforward: turn Bristol and its dissenting suburbs of Redcliffe, Temple and St Thomas into a county in its own right. It would then hold its own courts and be governed by a body of its own councillors.

So the King sent letters patent to the Bishops of Bath and Wells and Worcester, and to the Abbots of Cirencester and Glastonbury and to six neighbouring gentry to pace the boundary and erect stones of demarcation. The ceremony was performed on September 30th, 1374 and the whole transaction ratified by Parliament two months later. The first Mayor of the new County of Bristol was William Canynges a Redclivian.

The burgesses of Bristol had at last gained a resounding victory over the Lords of Berkeley, winning from them the rights of jurisdiction and assize that they had doggedly claimed for so long. It was a blow to the Berkeleys. With the forfeiture of Redcliffe and St Thomas it is claimed that they lost all chances of becoming one of the top ranking noble families in England. Yet Bristol's victory was not absolute. There was still one small, though niggling, thorn in the side of the new county – the Knights of St John of Jerusalem were to maintain independent control over Temple Fee for a good deal longer.

Notes
1.   F. Nichols and J. Taylor, *Bristol Past and Present* (Bristol, 1881) Vol 2, p.101
2.   Dermott Harding (ed.), *Bristol Charters 1155-1373* (Bristol Record Society, 1930) p.45
3.   S. Seyer, *Memoirs of Bristol* (Bristol, 1822) Vol 1, p.529
4.   Dermott Harding, op cit, p.1819
5.   M. Hebditch, *Excavations on the Medieval Defences, Portwall Lane Bristol* (Bristol and Gloucestershire Archaeological Society) Vol 87, p.135
6.   Seyer, *Memoirs of Bristol* (Bristol, 1823) Vol 11, p.38
7.   *Adam's Chronicle of Bristol* (Bristol, 1910) p.21
8.   J. Latimer, *Leland in Gloucestershire* (B.G.A.S., 1890) Vol 14, p.221
9.   R. Macaulay, *They Went to Portugal* (Penguin, 1985) p.25
10. J. Leech, *The Rural Rides of the Bristol Church Goer* (Gloucester, 1982) p.88
11. B. Williams, *Excavations in the Medieval Suburb of Bristol* (Bristol, 1981) p.5
12. S. Seyer, op cit, p.143
13. J. Sherbourne, *William Canynges 1402-1474* (Bristol Branch of the Historical Association, 1985) p.3
14. S. Seyer, op cit, p.81
15. ibid, p.81
16. J. Latimer, *Bristol Charters* (1909) p.68

Other Sources: W. Hunt, *Bristol* (London, 1889). J.W. Sherborne, *Port of Bristol in the Middle Ages* (1965). D. Walker, *Bristol in the Early Middle Ages* (1971)

TWO

THE GREAT MERCHANTS

The emergence of the woollen cloth trade was also accompanied by the rise of the great cloth merchants; wise and illustrious men such as Robert of Cheddar, Richard Le Spicer and, most famous of all, the Canynges family. They left an indelible mark, not only on the commercial records of Bristol, but also on the physical landscape.

The Canynges – no mere merchants but political figures whose influence spread as far as the King – were particularly associated with the Southern Parishes.

William (died 1396) and John Canynges (died c.1406) made their money mostly from the cloth trade both producing cloth and selling it in the established markets of Ireland, Gascony and the Iberian Peninsula. William Canynges the Younger (1402-1474) was even bolder in his enterprise. At a time when trade was generally poor he made a very courageous move. According to James Sherbourne he withdrew from personal shipments of wine and cloth and took to using his own ships for transportation of the goods of others.[1] In other words he established his own shipping line. It was a gamble, but a gamble that paid off. By 1460 William Canynges the Younger had his own fleet of nine ships and was said to employ a colossal workforce of eight hundred people; one in eight of the adult population in Bristol was in Canynges' employ. He was involved in more trade in northern Europe than anyone else in the country, dealing with the export of cloth, food and drink and the import of, among other things, dried and salted fish.

William Canynges the Younger was innovative in other ways. The pride of the Canynges' fleet was the giant 900 ton *Mary and John*, an absolute monster of a vessel when the average ship on the quay was only 200 tons.

The most successful merchants were also politicians. In Bristol they had to be if they were to get a fair share of the country's trade. William Canynges the Younger was five times Mayor of Bristol and twice represented the town in Parliament. Such was his power that when Henry VI pledged a protectionist treaty with the King of Denmark a special and unique licence was made excluding Canynges from the embargo.

We may know the names of Canynges' ships but of those who sailed in them we know nothing. This is one of the regrettable problems of medieval history; only a few exceptional characters are recorded – the everyday people, the mainstay of Bristol's maritime greatness, go unmentioned.

A unique and precise record does exist, however, of Bristol's medieval buildings.

The tomb of William Canynges (1402-1474), St Mary Redcliffe Church.
Canynges, a nationally influential merchant, was said to have
employed over 800 people. (Photo M. Manson)

William of Worcester, a scholar who had been in the service of Sir John Fastolf, a prominent landowner in East Anglia, retired to Bristol and spent his last years recording in remarkable detail the fabric of the town. He must have appeared an eccentric figure pacing the streets, noting down in his little book the measurements of buildings, streets and even the bridge. He was obsessed by numbers, often to the exclusion of any aesthetic detail.

Although the Southern Parishes had been incorporated into Bristol in 1373, Redcliffe, Temple and St Thomas retained a character and spirit of their own. The Southern Parishes still had a rural feel about them – animals freely roamed the streets and once outside the town walls you were immediately in the kingcup meadows of Temple and Redcliffe Meads. And even within the walls there was still plenty of space. The bigger houses had gardens and orchards, some of which ran down to the river. It was not until 1470 that the busy main thoroughfares of Redcliffe, Temple, Thomas and Tucker Streets were paved; before this they would have been impossibly muddy during wet weather and dusty during dry. Most houses were timber framed structures filled-in with wattle and daub and roofed with straw. There were exceptions though; the few people with money built with more permanent materials. Undoubtedly the most impressive private house in the Southern Parishes was William Canynges' residence in Redcliffe Street. Built of stone, it even broke away from the local vernacular styles by incorporating, as William of Worcester noted, 'baye wyndowes.'

The front rooms of Canynges' house looked out on Redcliffe Street, behind them stretched the great hall with its lofty roof supported on corbels carved in the shape of angels, and way beyond this, past two courtyards and many other rooms was a stone tower overlooking the river.[2] In an age when most buildings were of an insubstantial nature this one was made to last. Incredibly, high up in a wall just off Redcliffe Street there remain today two small splayed windows that must once have belonged to this very house. Apart from bits and pieces of the old castle this wall of Canynges' house must be one of the earliest secular fragments of Bristol to survive to the present day. In fact much of the structure of Canynges house remained until the 1930s when in a shameless act of vandalism the Great Hall and other buildings were torn down. Fortunately the tiled floor, reputedly laid for a visit of Edward IV when he was a guest of Canynges in 1461, was saved and is now in the British Museum.

The Canynges were a rich family and, like their fellow merchants in such a God fearing age, were anxious to make donations towards philanthropic enterprises and ecclesiastical funds. After all, the dreadful pestilence of 1349 and its frequent recurrence was a constant reminder of God's omnipotence. The plague was interpreted by many as a sign of God's displeasure and it was conjectured that such charitable acts as church building and the endowment of almshouses might go some way to appease this wrath. Thus Richard Le Spicer established his almshouse just inside Temple Gate in the 1350s whilst Simon De Burton's almshouse opposite St Thomas's church in Long Row, founded in 1292, had already been long built. Somewhat less orthodox was Thomas Berkeley's quest for salvation. In 1347 he installed a hermit, John Sparkes, in a cave in Redcliffe Pit (the cave can still be seen in the Garden for the Blind) to pray for his redemption.

The Canynges family, along with other merchants, inaugurated a massive rebuilding scheme for St Mary Redcliffe. Over three generations the church was transformed from a small Norman chapel, an outlier of the Bedminster parish church, to the flower of perpendicular architecture, the 'pride of Bristowe and the Western land', that we know today.

The rebuilding in mellow Dundry stone started in earnest at the beginning of the fourteenth century when William Canynges the Elder and other citizens demolished most of the Norman structure and commenced the present building on the same site. The transformation took many years and evidence of a temporary roof indicates the suspension of the project for a while. In 1445 when the church was nearing completion there was a serious and most unexpected setback. During a violent thunderstorm the spire, nearly 300 feet of it, was struck by lightning. Blown by a strong west wind it came crashing down through the nave ruining a large part of the building. Rather than discourage Canynges this disaster merely inspired him to greater beneficence; he moved in a workforce of over one hundred people – masons, carpenters and labourers – to get on with the job. Eventually, the church was practically completed by 1480. The damaged nave was repaired but the steeple remained unfinished. For the next four hundred years the parishioners had to be content with a splendid gilded weathercock as a crown to the church's sadly truncated spire.

The church of St Thomas the Martyr was also closely connected with the Canynges family. Several generations of the family were buried there. The church itself – not the one we have today – was described by William Barrett as 'next to Redcliffe, the largest as well as the most elegant building.'[3] This was no mean compliment. Unfortunately we have little other evidence to confirm Barret's opinion as no detailed or specific picture of the early church survives.

William Canynges died, leaving no direct heir, six years before the building work on St Mary Redcliffe was concluded. His life being inextricably linked with St Mary Redcliffe, it comes as no surprise that his death in 1474, at the age of 72, is commemorated in the church. What is unusual though is that his memory is marked by not one altar tomb but two. Both tombs are placed in the south transept: one depicts Canynges in mayoral robes lying next to his wife, whilst the other represents him in the clothes of a priest. He has the features, wrote Bryan Little, 'of a Quaker business man...a devout and austere cleric.'[4]

The two tombs can be explained easily, as for the last seven years of his life Canynges turned his back on the world of commerce and sought holy orders. Records indicate that within days of the death of his wife, Joan, he entered the priesthood. One small shadow, however, hangs over the details of this retirement. In Ricart's Calendar there is a curious entry for 1466 which states '...Mr Canynges should have been married by the King's command wherefore he in all haste took orders...'[5] This is indeed strange for apart from the Calendar which was written a long time after the event no other record exists to support this statement. Without further evidence it is perhaps best to take the view of the Victorian historian, Dallaway and dismiss this part of Ricart's writing as merely 'a silly tradition of malicious rumour.'

William Canynges eventually became Dean of Westbury College, a few miles north of Bristol. (It was from Westbury that the more austere of the two Redcliffe tombs came, being transferred when the college was dissolved in 1544.) It was a fitting retirement for someone who had publicly led such a devout life. And even today the event is commemorated in St Mary Redcliffe at Whitsun by the charming Rush Sunday service.

DECLINE OF THE WOOLLEN INDUSTRY

The impetus of growth of the woollen manufacturing industry in the Southern Parishes did not last. As elsewhere in England, the woollen industry in Bristol was moving to the countryside where it could escape the stifling control of the guilds and also take advantage in Gloucestershire of the swift running water of the steep-sided Cotswold valleys. This slow demise was a reflection of what was happening nationally to urban cloth manufacture.

But not only was the industry deserting the parishes of Redcliffe, Temple and St Thomas. In 1453 there was also a major shift of market when England lost its long cherished hold on Gascony. From then on the merchants of Bristol had to seek out new customers in Spain and Portugal. Luckily both these areas, like Gascony, produced strong wines to which the English palate was partial and which could be imported in return for the export of cloth.

Apart from the Iberian Peninsula, the loss of Gascony encouraged Bristolians to look even further afield for new markets. Through their voyages to Iceland they were as familiar with the tempestuous Atlantic as anybody else; it therefore seemed entirely natural that they should turn their attention to the mysteries of what lay beyond and try to discover a new way to the riches of the Orient.

As Spain, by treaty, had already annexed the Southern Hemisphere all explorers from England had to sail northwards.

In reality the finding of the new world must have been a bewildering disappointment. What the Genoese John Cabot and his Bristol born son Sebastian found when they got to the other side of the Atlantic Ocean in 1497, one year before Christopher Columbus discovered South America, was a damp, misty, altogether uninviting continent. The navigators came back to Bristol not with valuable spices but with more cod and also little

Drawn & Engraved by Ethel Blore

St Mary Redcliffe: for four hundred years the parishioners had to be content with a sadly truncated spire.

Simon De Burton's Almshouse. One of Bristol's earliest almshouses. Established in 1292 for the relief of 16 poor or aged women. By 1570 the almshouses were described as being in such a bad state of repair 'that in a short time they will come to extreme ruin if a remedy is not provided.' The buildings survived, however, until the blitz of 1940. (City of Bristol Museum and Art Gallery)

immediate chance of a new market for the cloth industry. In Bristol's case the important discoveries of the New World were slow to bear fruit.

The loss of the woollen cloth market was, however, only a temporary setback. Trading relations were soon re-established when the Gascons realised that they needed a market for their wines as much as the West Country needed a market for their cloth. In fact by the end of the fifteenth century, Bristol was exporting three times as much cloth as in the period 1400-1420.[6] The difference was, however, that little of this cloth came from the Southern Parishes. The cloth market may have re-established itself, but in the process, right across the country, it had moved its manufacturing base from the towns to the countryside.

REFORMATION OF THE CHURCH

Changes were also being brought about through the reformation of the church. This reformation, which had been going on for many years – the Protestant leader Latimer is reported to have preached in St Thomas church in 1528 – was hastened by Henry VIII's own personal dispute with Rome. As Bristol was virtually surrounded by ecclesiastical land, Henry VIII's dissolution of the monasteries between 1536 and 1540 opened up new opportunities for development. The Parliament of 1540 passed, with little opposition, a bill that granted to the King all the lands, goods and houses of the abbeys, priories, nunneries and chantries that had been, or were about to be, suppressed. Subsequently Henry VIII – ever short of money due to his extravagant and fruitless campaigns in France – sold these for knock-down prices. In South Bristol the Corporation, though lacking in funds, was keen to buy the Hospital of St John in Redcliffe Pit, just outside Redcliffe Gate.

St John's Hospital, founded by the Berkeleys in the late twelfth century for the aid of the sick and the dying, was a small establishment of a hall, cloisters with a fountain fed by the Redcliffe pipe and outbuildings. It had a somewhat uneventful history. Perhaps its main claim to fame was that Henry VI stayed there whilst visiting Bristol in 1446. Although merely a stone's throw across the road from St Mary Redcliffe its connections with the fine church are limited. St Mary Redcliffe was in the diocese of Salisbury whilst St John's Hospital came under the control of the Bishop of Wells. A strict agreement was made between the Hospital and St Mary Redcliffe that they should not poach each other's clientele.[7]

The Corporation was not immediately able to purchase St John's Hospital as Henry VIII had already granted it to his physician, George Owen. In 1553, however, Dr Owen granted a 99 year lease to the Corporation of numerous houses across the city belonging to the hospital and some time later granted them the hospital itself.

The Dissolution had other, more unexpected effects. For a start it put an end to the long disputed independence of Temple Fee. Even as late as 1532 the Corporation of Bristol, claiming that Temple Fee was a lawless area and a refuge for outlaws, had been contesting the authority of the Knights of St John of Jerusalem to exercise a jurisdiction independent of the city of Bristol. This trouble with the Knights came to an abrupt end with the Dissolution.

More surprising, perhaps, was what happened to St Thomas Church. It had to change its name. By statute it was ordered that 'St Thomas of Canterbury should not be esteemed or called a saint: that all images of him should be destroyed, the festival in his honour be abolished, and his name and remembrance be erased out of all books under pain of his majesty's indignation and imprisonment at his grace's pleasure.'[8]

Accordingly by 1566 we find that Apostle has been substituted for Martyr.

POVERTY AND PLAGUE

The closure of St John's Hospital was yet another blow for the poor of South Bristol. By 1570, it was written that: 'The houses, structures and edifices are reduced to such a state of ruin and decay to the great nuisance to that part of the city; and the late inhabitants being forced by want, through the decay in their trade in making woollen cloths have suffered their homes to go to ruin; and that a certain almshouse situated near the said street for the support of many poor, and also a certain canal or pipe of water situated there which beyond the memory of man has been supported and maintained by the said inhabitants, are now in such a state on account of their poverty, that in a short time they will come to extreme ruin, if a remedy is not provided...'[9]

Also Simon De Burton's almshouse was becoming dilapidated and perhaps more serious, the conduit, St Thomas' main source of water, was in bad repair. This decline is clearly emphasised in the parish returns of 1544 and 1574 which show a predominant position of wealth in the central parishes of Bristol to the north of the bridge. The Southern Parishes were no longer fashionable; there was a feeling of malaise in the air; the days when the wealthy merchants clamoured to live to the south of the Avon were long gone.

What could be done to revitalise the area? By 1570 matters were so bad that the Corporation took the very positive step of introducing a weekly market to strengthen the parishes' economy. The market, to be held on Thursdays, was for the sale of 'yarn cloth, cattle and all other things whatsoever.' With the money generated it was expected that the parish of St Thomas 'may be better able to support and maintain' its houses, its almshouses and its conduit.

The grant of a market expressed a radical change in the thinking of the Corporation. Only thirty years before, extreme disapproval had been shown of another trading venture, the Candlemas Fair at Redcliffe. This fair had been held for thirteen years when the traditional rivalries between north and south brought it to an end. The people of the northern parishes complained, probably with some justification, that traders were only coming to the town at Candlemas to avoid tolls that would have been paid at any other time. Despite a petition of support bearing 629 signatures to the Star Chamber the Mayor had his way and in 1542 the Candlemas Fair was abandoned.[10]

However, after the tariff on gate-entry was abolished in 1546, the St Thomas market was looked upon as less of a threat and, indeed, became a more permanent affair; it was held regularly every Thursday until 1840 when it was transferred to Temple Meads.

Once the market was established, the vestry of the church got to work to build a rudimentary shelter for some of the more perishable products. A flat topped roof supported by stone pillars was constructed along the eastern side of the church of St Thomas. Many years later in 1691 four posts with brass caps upon them similar to the famous and supposedly unique Nails in Corn Street were donated for the telling of money.[11]

Although the Tudor era is generally regarded as the end of the Middle Ages and the dawn of modern times it is doubtful whether the people of the Southern Parishes noticed any such difference. The plague certainly had lost none of its potency and its occurrence was just as frequent. There are records of its presence in Bristol in 1544, 1551, 1564, 1574 and at the beginning of the seventeenth century it appeared in Bristol five times in only eight years. Obviously the authorities were keen to take steps to avoid the spread of this dreadful pestilence, but with limited knowledge of medical science it was difficult.

It was believed that the plague was carried by tiny creatures which infected the air making it denser than normal; dirty, dark and damp places were where these creatures could be found. To dispel the infection, enormous fires were lit in the streets, bells rung and cannons discharged to break up the density of the air. Precautions against the plague such as the wearing of amulets, the carrying of nosegays and the anointing of houses with oil were popular. It was advisable to remain cheerful at all times whilst music to dispel bad dreams was also recommended.

Fortunately there was at least some concept of quarantine though not through any sound scientific reason. Travellers from areas of the country known to be affected were subjected, along with their possessions, to a lengthy 'air' before admission to the city. The house of anyone infected by plague was boarded up with the occupants still inside. Those confined were given charitable relief and fed at the expense of the city. A watchman was also stationed outside to prevent entrance or exit. A cutler of St Thomas Street who contracted the illness in 1603 was accordingly imprisoned in such a manner. This course of action was unpopular and mostly ineffective. Householders were slow to report cases of infection and, indeed, would often disappear elsewhere before the outbreak was discovered by the authorities. Consequently the plague spread even further afield.

The beginning of the seventeenth century also brought with it the additional problems of particularly severe weather conditions. In 1606 there was an enormous flood when the lower part of the city was inundated. In Redcliffe, Temple and Thomas streets the water was as 'high as mens girdles', and in Temple and Thomas churches it was 'half way up the seats.'[12] At Treen Mills, (now the site of the Bathurst Basin) where the Malago Stream, or Bedminster Brook as it was then known, entered the Avon, the flood water was five feet deep. The following winter the whole country was gripped by a severe and prolonged frost. Unlike the Thames which at Westminster froze right over, the Avon with its large tidal fall remained free flowing. The streets however were slippery and dangerous. 'During this frost everyman was forced to strew stonecoal ashes before their doors to save the men and horses from falling; and the mayor sent about the bellman to command everyman to dig up ice and snow and cast it upon heaps and haul it away and over the Backe and the Quay.'[13]

In spite of the efforts of the Thomas Street market, hardship continued. Bristol had an additional problem with vagrants who came across the sea from Ireland looking for work. Every so often these sturdy beggars were rounded up, caged in the Newgate Gaol and then shipped back to their mother country in 'a drove.'

Although the Irish vagrants were treated harshly there was a more sympathetic approach for the local poor. Vagrancy and poverty were national problems in the Tudor period. There was, however, a new more enlightened approach as it was beginning to be understood that poor relief was not just encumbent on charities and the church but on society as a whole. The law was beginning to recognise that there were different categories of poor – the sick, the old, the insane or those just temporarily down on their luck. In 1601 a new statute relating to poor relief was introduced which specified that overseers for the poor in every parish were to buy material to provide work for the unemployed. This statute was implemented locally in 1617 and 1618 when the Corporation opened a house in Temple Street for the employment of children in the manufacture of Kersey.

VISIT OF QUEEN ELIZABETH 1

Poverty, plague and climatic hardship aside, there were times for celebration. One such occasion was the visit of Queen Elizabeth to the city in 1574. Although we know that the parish of St Thomas – amongst others – was down at heel this did not hinder the Corporation from pulling out all the stops to entertain the monarch. An unprecedented £1,000 was spent on the preparations, pageants and decorations; £200 of this being spent on gunpowder alone.

Statue of Elizabeth I in St Mary Redcliffe. On her visit to Bristol in 1574 the Queen confirmed what every Redclivian had always known – that their church was the fairest in the land. (Photo M.Manson)

The roads were sanded and repaired, burgesses were given new uniforms and preparations were made for the novelty of the visit, the mock battle which was to be held on the Addercliffe (now the site of Redcliffe Parade) and below at Treen Mills. The entertainments were coordinated by the enthusiastic John Churchyard who saw to it that the Queen was met wherever she went by young men who would welcome her in elaborate verse. The Elizabethan age is justly famed for its lyrical verse, unfortunately, in the words of John Latimer, this was 'tedious rhymned twaddle.' Indeed the speeches were delivered with more enthusiasm than they were received: several of the young orators were cut off in mid soliloquy on the pretext that time was short.

The undisputed highlight of the visit was the staging of the mock battle on the scrubby Addercliffe. A scaffold was built across the river on the edge of the Marsh (now Queen Square) for viewing and over an exhausting three day period a war was waged. In fact it was enacted with such ferocity that several of the participants were injured. The battle was not only a display of military prowess, it also contained an allegorical message for Her Majesty about her dealings with the Spanish – a fort called 'Feble Pollecie' was quickly attacked and demolished. (In later years, when there was a real threat of a Spanish invasion, Addercliffe was used for the more serious purpose of mustering able bodied men in readiness for attack by the Armada.)

With all the excitement engendered by the royal visit it would seem that the care taken in the storage of the gunpowder to be used in the mock battle was slipshod. A day before the Queen's arrival some of the explosives, which were being kept at the Pelican Inn in St Thomas Street, ignited. In the explosion that followed five people were killed, another ten injured and the inn devastated. Further mishaps followed; 'about as many men were likewise burned by misfortune with gunpowder at Treene Mills.'

Apart from the accidents, the Queen's visit was a popular success. Surprisingly, it is by a casual remark attributed to Queen Elizabeth that she is most remembered in Bristol today. For in one sentence the Monarch confirmed what every true Redclivian had always believed: that their church, St Mary's, was the 'fairest, godliest and most famous Parish Church in England.'

Notes

1.   J. Sherborne, *William Canynges* (Bristol, 1985) p.9
2.   J. Dallaway, *Antiquities of Bristol* (Bristol, 1834) p.145-146
3.   W. Barrett, *The History and the Antiquities of Bristol* (Bristol, 1789) p.558
4.   B. Little, *City and County of Bristol* (Bristol, 1954) p.85
5.   *Adam's Chronicle of Bristol* (Bristol, 1910) p.70
6.   J. Sherborne, *The Port of Bristol in the Middle Ages* (Bristol, 1971) p.21-22
7.   G. Parker, *The History of the Hospital of St.John the Baptist. Redcliff Pit* (Bristol, 1925)
8.   J. F. Nichols and J. Taylor *Bristol Past and Present* (Bristol, 1882) Vol 2, p.230-232
9.   W. Barrett, op. cit, p.565
10. J. Vanes, *The Port of Bristol in the Sixteenth Century,* p.19
11. W. Barrett, op. cit, p.565
12. S. Seyer, *Memoirs of Bristol,* (1823) Vol 2, p.260
13. Adams, op. cit, p.183-184

Other Sources

J. Evans, *A Chronological Outline of the History of Bristol* (Bristol, 1824)
J. Latimer, *Sixteenth Century Bristol* (Bristol, 1908)
R. Latham, *Bristol Charters—1509-1899* (Bristol, 1947)
M. D. Lobel, E. M. Carus-Wilson, *Bristol* (London, 1975)
K. G. Porting, *The Woollen Industry of South West England* (Bath, 1971)
E. N. Simmons, *Into Unknown Waters: John and Sebastian Cabot* (London, 1964)
I. Wilson, *The Columbus Myth* (London, 1991)

THREE

THE INVINCIBLE PORTWALL

It was more by quirk of fate than design that Bristol found itself in support of the Parliamentary cause at the beginning of the Civil War. Indeed, like much of the country, the city would have preferred to stay neutral, for what use was a civil war – a war of ideas at that – to the merchants and traders of Bristol?

However, the protagonists of the war thought otherwise. Bristol, as second city in the country, would be of vital importance to whoever finally ruled England. The city was far too influential to be left alone.

So, with the arrival in Bristol of Colonel Essex, a Parliamentary figurehead and Governor of Gloucester, a neutral stance was no longer possible. Essex and his army marched into Bristol in 1642 and, with little opposition and no bloodshed, the city found itself host to the Roundhead garrison. For Bristol the Civil War was just beginning.

By the following spring, as the King's followers gained strength in the West Country, it became obvious that the city would soon be under attack. Preparations were made for the defence of the city. In the Southern Parishes cannons were mounted at strategic positions; Temple Gate and the easternmost bastion, Tower Harratz, had fourteen cannons between them, while in the vicinity of Redcliffe there were another fifteen. To the north of the Avon, however, the fortifications were more haphazard. Colonel Fiennes, the new Governor who had taken over from Colonel Essex who had been found to be drunk and unreliable, reluctantly admitted that 'Bristol was one of the hardest towns to be fortified.'

On Sunday July 23rd, Prince Rupert, the 24-year old nephew of King Charles, and his army set up quarters a couple of miles outside the city, at Westbury-on-Trym.

A little before dawn on the following Wednesday the attack on the city began. The Cornish Royalists were assigned the unenviable task of assailing the Portwall. They began their thrust at 3.00 am – earlier than planned; an act that has been interpreted by some as eagerness but by others as dissatisfaction with being allocated such a difficult task. It was a short but determined attack. Against all odds the Cornishmen fought with 'a courage and resolution that nothing but death can control.'[1] Their first task was to fill the defensive ditch by driving carts into it. But the ditch proved deeper than expected, it was only at Temple Gate that some of the assailants were able to mount the city wall and even then they were quickly repelled. After half an hour of fighting, when 'the bodies lay on the ground like rotten sheep,'[2] the Cornishmen retreated under a hail of bullets and stones to the safety of the hedgerows of Temple and Redcliffe Meads. Their losses were needlessly high as across the city, to the north of the river, the defences, although proving stronger than expected, with time were inevitably breached.

Thankfully there were no large-scale massacres with the fall of the city – this was perhaps a reflection of the lack of commitment by Bristolians to any one side. Relationships between Royalists and Parliamentarians were as cordial as the conditions of war would permit. Indeed, the city fathers were as much concerned by the empty ships in the harbour and the loss of trade as they were with anything else. 'The governing body' as Patrick McGrath wrote 'would have preferred to adopt a policy of non-involvement. When this proved impossible it cooperated without much fuss with whatever garrison occupied the city'[3].

Certainly with the fall of Bristol to the Royalists there were no reported atrocities. But there was plundering. The shops on the bridge suffered most with the excuse that shopkeepers there harboured a particular hatred for the cavaliers.

The surrender of Bristol was seen as 'a fulltide of prosperity for the King.' But the victory cost him dear: 500 men fell in the assault.

The King's good fortune was short lived. Victory at Bristol was followed by a disastrous and unsuccessful siege at Gloucester. From then onwards the Royalists lost ground and by June 1645, after the battle of Naseby, the King held only the West of England. By the end of July, when the Royalists had lost Somerset and hardly had a field army to speak of, the capture of Bristol was seen by the Parliamentarians as a foregone conclusion.

Prince Rupert, however, had other ideas and certainly hoped that Bristol would evade capture. Since Fiennes' defeat Prince Rupert's garrison of 4,500 men had worked hard to improve the city's fortifications. In a letter to the King he felt confident enough to state that he had provisions and ammunition to last a long siege, moreover, with the unseasonal wet and cold weather he knew that the morale of the Roundheads was low. To play on their low spirits Prince Rupert harassed the besiegers with sudden attacks on their dispersed forces. One of several such spirited forays by the Cavaliers was a sally from Temple Gate into the Roundheads' Bedminster Camp; the Parliamentarians were caught unawares with ten people killed and a similar number taken hostage.

On September 6th, Cromwell dined in the fields near St Mary Redcliffe and reconnoitred the strong southern defences. To attract as little attention as possible the soldiers were ordered not to salute their general.

Bristol's defences – stretching four miles in all – might have been strengthened by Rupert's army, but the northern fortifications, twisting up and down the hills required a large number of soldiers to cover them adequately. Knowing this, Cromwell and Fairfax decided upon a swift all out attack rather than a lengthy siege.

For over two weeks Prince Rupert played for time with hesitant negotiations, but by September 9th, Cromwell could stand the procrastination no longer and ordered the attack to begin at one in the morning of the following day.

Despite the obvious invincibility of the Portwall the attack upon it was fierce. Three 'forlorn hopes,' each of two hundred men, were to lead the storm. This time the attackers brought ladders to scale the walls, but they misjudged the height and the ladders proved too short. They were quickly repulsed with a loss of one hundred men. Predictably the earth works to the north of the city proved to be the weak link and by evening Prince Rupert had surrendered.

The surrender was negotiated in a most gentlemanly manner. Rupert and his army were allowed to leave Bristol and were given eight days' freedom of passage to a garrison of their own choice. On the next day, September 11th, Rupert left the Royal Fort at Kingsdown for Oxford with '8 lords in his company, 500 horse and 1400 foot with their muskets and other arms.'[4] Fairfax accompanied him for two miles over Durdham Down and 'treated him with great courtesy.'[5]

The loss of Bristol to the Roundheads, in reality, indicated the end of the King's fight for England. Incensed at his nephew's conduct and overwhelmed by the loss, Charles wrote to Rupert reproaching him for 'submitting to so mean an action.' The King reminded Rupert of his letter 'whereby you assured me that if no mutiny happened you would keep Bristol for four months. Did you keep it four days? Was there anything like a mutiny?'[6] The King concluded his letter by dismissing Rupert from his service and ordering him to quit the country.

When Cromwell and Fairfax entered Bristol they were surprised by what they saw. With a large number of soldiers garrisoned in the city conditions had deteriorated. The plague had also been raging for some months. 'It looked more like a prison than a city and the people more like prisoners than citizens being brought so low by taxation, so poor in habit and so dejected in countenance; the streets so noisome and the houses so nasty that they were unfit to receive friends or freemen until they were cleansed.'[7]

With the fighting over, soldiers from the garrison visited the parish churches and destroyed what they called 'idolatrous sculpture.'[8] Included in the term was stained glass; in St Mary Redcliffe this was almost entirely smashed. Organs, which were also seen as 'objects illegal in the worship of God' were pulled down. The organ pipes of St Mary Redcliffe were carried through the streets and blown as trumpets.

Meanwhile, Prince Rupert followed the King to Newark, where he appealed against his expulsion from the country. A council of war subsequently found the Prince not guilty of treachery or cowardice but censured him for negligence.

The King surrendered in May 1646 – he was beheaded in London before a silent crowd on January 30th, 1649.

SOLEMNITY AND SERIOUSNESS

Although the 1640s and 1650s were a period of expanding horizons for Bristol's overseas trade, at home there was a contraction of freedoms and a stifling of many activities that had always been taken for granted. This was the age of the Puritan: 'a narrow spirited, bigoted and fanatical age' when Bristolians found that many of their pleasures were banned or made illegal. It was a time of solemnity and seriousness; profane language was punishable by the stocks, Christmas Day was for fasting and to walk on the Sabbath, even to collect water, was a crime.

Puritan bigotry was at its worst when it came to the toleration of other religious groups. Indicative of these feelings was a bill read in Parliament in September 1646 stating that Unitarians and heretics could be put to death and Baptists and other sectarians jailed. In Bristol, the Quakers were constantly harassed. Particularly distressing was the treatment of the 'mad messiah,' James Naylor.

Before his arrival in Bristol, Naylor had been touring the West Country claiming to be a reincarnation of Christ. Although obviously mentally disturbed he was a charismatic figure and attracted a group of dedicated supporters. When Naylor arrived in Bristol in 1646, to the horror of the Puritan leaders, he was met at Redcliffe Gate by cries of rejoicing and hosannas. He was promptly arrested and sent to London to be tried for blasphemy. To the Puritans his guilt was in no doubt; difficulties arose, however, in devising a suitable chastisement. Finally, after thirteen days' deliberation, a sentence was declared which though it avoided execution was as cruel and gruesome as can be imagined. Two hours in the pillory at Westminster was to be followed by Naylor having his tongue severed through with a red hot iron and his forehead branded with a B. And this was only the beginning: he was then to be sent to Bristol to ride through the streets bareback and be whipped in St Thomas Street market and other parts of the city. Finally, it was proposed that he be returned to London and earn his living by hard labour in solitary confinement.

This punishment, authorised by Parliament without a voice raised against it, shocked the people of Bristol. The Mayor and other influential citizens presented a petition for remission but it was to no avail and the sentence was carried out.[9]

James Naylor claimed to belong to the Quakers, one of the new religious groups that arose out of the spiritual fervour engendered around the time of the Civil War. Very simply the Quakers advocated an absolutely spiritual approach to God unhindered by all the earthly trappings that went with the established church. Churches and priests, they argued, only served to distract attention away from, rather than focus on God. The foundation of Quakerism is dated to 1652 and is first recorded in Bristol in 1654. From that date onwards the city became a centre for Quakerism in the South West. A perturbed commentator wrote in 1660: 'these monsters are more numerous in Bristol

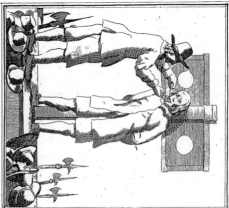

The Mad Messiah, James Naylor, was sentenced in 1646 to have his tongue severed with a red-hot iron, his forehead branded with a B and then to be whipped though the streets.

than the rest of the West Country, and hold meetings of 1,000 or 1,200 to the great alarm of the city.'

Though not officially outlawed during the period of the Commonwealth, the Quakers' strict lifestyle, their hatred of hypocrisy, their emotional and outspoken behaviour and their so-called lack of respect for authority made them targets for attack. Certainly the Quakers' popularity was hardly increased by their compulsion to interrupt Anglican church services and harangue both the 'hireling' priests, as they called them, and the congregation. Matters were also not helped by the brazen arrival in Bristol of the deranged James Naylor. Consequently, as the Quakers went about the city, they were, in the words of a contemporary writer (1660) 'openly abused, reproached, dirtied, stoned, pinched, kicked and grossly injured'[10]. It is as well to remember, however, that half a century before they would have been burnt at the stake.

Some Quakers, like William Penn, the son of Admiral Sir William Penn, went to America to find their peace – many more stayed in England.

Although the Quakers held no formal church services they did need accommodation for their meetings. So they established a Meeting House first of all in 1656 to the north of the Avon, in Broadmead, and then another in 1667 in Temple Street. They also purchased land in 1665 for a burial ground in Redcliffe Pit (still there, a quiet, secluded spot opposite St Mary Redcliffe Church on Redcliffe Hill).

Of course a society of strict conformity such as there was during the Commonwealth era must have its releases. One such safety valve was provided by the traditional festivals which offered a time of institutionalised disorder. Of these, the Shrove Tuesday festivities were celebrated with particular glee; whatever was lacking in the even more austere days of Lent was emphasised in that day's revelries. Amongst the most popular customs of the day were the sadistic games of cock throwing and dog tossing. Indeed, on Shrove Tuesday, it was dangerous to walk down some of the streets for fear of being hit by the shower of missiles flung at hapless cocks. These birds were tied by the leg and anyone willing to pay a penny was allowed to throw, from a distance, a stick or stone at it, the bird being theirs if it was killed. The nature of dog tossing is even more obscure. The diarist Samuel Pepys wrote in 1666 about dogs being tossed by bulls and commented that 'it is a very rude and nasty pleasure.' The present day substitute of a pancake is certainly preferable.

Needless to say, the Puritans found these Shrove Tuesday revelries offensive and in 1655 tried to ban them. The prohibition was ignored, however, and the 'sports' continued as usual. Equally ineffectual was a renewed ban in 1660. When the bellman attempted on March 5th (the day before Shrove Tuesday) to announce the outlawing of the 'sport' he was set upon, beaten and had the livery torn off his back. But the next day the law was obeyed to the very letter. Certainly there was no cock throwing or dog tossing – for the animals had been changed to hens, geese, cats and bitches. The youths took particular delight in their hen throwing and bitch tossing, carrying on with their fun directly outside the Mayor's house. A sheriff who tried to put a stop to this insult had his 'head broken for his labour.'[11]

Although the illegal celebrations were a minor protest they nevertheless indicate a growing disenchantment with the Puritan regime.

Nationally there was a feeling that Parliamentary rule must soon come to an end. Oliver Cromwell had died in 1658 and his son, Tumbledown Dick as he was called, proved an unworthy successor. The belief was slowly growing that the country would be safer in the hands of a monarch responsible to Parliament rather than armies answerable only to themselves.

So, just two months after the Shrove Tuesday riots, Charles II was rapturously welcomed off the ship, the Naseby, at Dover and a few days later proclaimed as King in London. For the first time in twenty years the people of England looked forward to a new found security. At least one thing was quickly restored to normal: having held their tongues for so long the people were once again able to give voice to strong language without fear of reprisal. Even Pepys, a man not noted for mincing his words, described the New Parliament of 1661 as 'the most profane, swearing fellows that I have ever heard in my life.'

On the other hand, Bristolians had found much that was admirable in the strict Puritan way of life; the dedication to hard work and the seriousness of intent were features that were attractive to Bristolian businesspeople and were not to be quickly abandoned.

BRISTOL'S FORGOTTEN HERO

Accompanying Charles II on the Naseby on his triumphant return to England in 1660 was Admiral Sir William Penn – one of the most distinguished Bristolians of the seventeenth century.

Born in Bristol and christened in St Thomas Church, Penn joined the Navy at an early age and by the time he was 21 was captain of his own ship. In his portrait that hangs in the Painted Hall at Greenwich his looks – he was short, round faced, and sandy haired – belie his ambition. His rise through the ranks was meteoric and his career far reaching. Penn fought the Dutch in the North Sea (he was also commander of the troops, the only man ever to hold the dual role of Admiral and General), he hunted the exiled Prince Rupert in the Mediterranean and climaxed his career in the West Indies where, in a stunning and bloodless victory, he annexed Jamaica as an English Colony.

Although during the Civil War Penn was seen to support the Parliamentary side this was due more to his scheming ambition than to any personal commitment to Roundhead ideals. As he was to prove in later life, Penn was always a Royalist at heart.

The tale of Penn's battle with the Dutch under the command of Admiral Blake is in the best swashbuckling tradition. When the Dutch Admiral Van Tromp fixed a broom to the mast of his ship to imply that he would sweep the English fleet from the Channel, Penn retaliated by hoisting a riding whip above the rigging to warn the Dutch that they were due for a good thrashing. It was not an idle threat; after three days' fight the Dutch were beaten.

It was with the capture of Jamaica that Penn really made his mark. The assault upon the island was, in fact, an afterthought. Admiral Penn and the commander of the troops, General Venables, had been dispatched to 'assault the spaniard' on Hispaniola (now Haiti). Though Penn carried out his duties as required, Venables bungled his part and the English force withdrew from Hispaniola empty handed.

Fearing an ignominious return to England after such a profitless venture, Penn and Venables focused their attention on Jamaica. This island was far easier prey. On May 16th, 1655 Penn sailed into what is now known as Kingston Harbour and within a week, with only minor skirmishes, the island was captured. After staying six weeks to see that good order had been established, Penn and Venables set off to England hopeful of a hero's welcome.

The capture of Jamaica, a sugar island which was soon to be a crucial base for the expansion of trade through the West Indies, was an important colonial triumph for both Bristol and the country as a whole. But far from receiving acclamation on their return, Penn and Venables were unexpectedly imprisoned in the Tower of London. Why? Had Cromwell discovered Penn's royalist tendencies? Was it because of the failure to capture Hispaniola? Or was it, perhaps, to cool the heels of both Penn and Venables who had had a personal dispute during the trip. The reason for the arrest has never been made clear.

Penn was detained in the Tower for six weeks and on release promptly retired from public life to his estate in Ireland. From there, no doubt provoked by his harsh treatment, he opened up correspondence with the royalists.

With the restoration of the monarchy in 1660 Charles II knighted Penn in gratitude for his support and also appointed him as commissioner for the Navy. In Penn's employ at the Admiralty was no less a person than Samuel Pepys. It has to be said that Pepys had a low regard for Penn, but the diarist, being an ambitious man himself, found it to his advantage to keep relations as cordial as possible. In his diary however, Pepys never misses a chance to vilify the Admiral. He frequently describes Penn as a 'false rogue' or a 'very villain' and constantly complains of his tight-fistedness. Pepys wrote that the food at Penn's house was of miserly proportions and on one memorable occasion he was served by Penn with 'a damned venison pasty that stank like a devil.'[12]

It wasn't only Pepys who disliked Penn. Although the fruits of his victories were popular, Penn as a man was not. This was especially so in Bristol. Indeed he failed to be elected as member of Parliament for the city in 1660 and after his death, at the age of 49, in 1670, the Bristol Corporation refused to participate in his funeral ceremony at St Mary Redcliffe.

Naval historians rank Penn's achievements alongside those of Nelson, Blake and Rodney, yet today the City of Bristol does little to honour his memory. The only tangible reminders of this eminent Bristolian are his trophies – rotting flags, gauntlets and an age blackened breast plate that is reputed to have been worn by Penn during the capture of Jamaica – which hang largely forgotten, high up in the nave of St Mary Redcliffe.

MONMOUTH THREATENS BRISTOL…
EXECUTIONS ON REDCLIFFE HILL

The ill-fated West Country rebellion of 1685 was far from glorious. Indeed, today it is remembered more than anything else for the retribution that followed.

With the intention of wresting the crown from the widely disliked James II, the Duke of Monmouth landed in Lyme Bay on June 11th, 1685. Already popular from previous exploits in the West, Monmouth, a bastard son of Charles II, was enthusiastically received during his march from the Dorset coast to Taunton. There, after a triumphant entry into the town, he was proclaimed King. From Taunton he moved to Bridgwater, and then on to Glastonbury, Wells and Shepton Mallet. The local support and loyalty that the dashing Duke received was remarkable; such dedication was unlike anything seen before – even during the years of the Civil War. All along the way his army swelled with excited volunteers, but despite this encouraging support Monmouth was perturbed. Few influential people had joined his cause. In reality his army comprised a peasant rabble.

Monmouth knew that if he was to hold any real influence in the West he would have to capture Bristol. This he was told would be an easy victory for he had been assured that there were thousands of sympathisers within the city.

There was little point in approaching Bristol from the south as the Portwall fortifications were known through the experience of the Civil War to be strong enough to withstand the most powerful attack. It was therefore decided to circumambulate the city and advance from the north. Ignorant of this plan the Duke of Beaufort had drawn up his troops outside Redcliffe Gate in readiness for battle. Suddenly, a pall of smoke was seen rising from the Quay. A ship was burning, the handiwork, it was surmised, of Monmouth's partisans. Equal to such skullduggery, the Duke of Beaufort forbade any of his men to leave their posts to fight the fire in case it was a diversion. Furthermore, to show that he meant business, he declared that if the inhabitants attempted any insurrection he would personally see that the city was incinerated about their ears.

Beaufort need not have worried, as evidence suggests that the burning boat was an accident unrelated to the revolt. Monmouth, meanwhile, was still pondering his plans while camped several miles away at Keynsham. On the night of June 24th, while

Monmouth's forces were idling, a small group of horseguards dashed into the camp and caused a general panic amongst the bucolic insurgents. This minor attack was the first real resistance that Monmouth had encountered, yet it so disturbed him that he lost his nerve and abandoned his half hearted designs on Bristol.

So Monmouth's disillusioned army straggled back to Bridgwater. On July 6th, the rebels, equipped largely with makeshift weapons such as billhooks and sickles, along with a few spears, were miserably defeated on the damp flats of Sedgemoor. It was the last battle to be fought on English soil. Monmouth lost all credibility by deserting his loyal followers before the end of the fray. He was captured a few days later in the New Forest, and after pleading in front of the King for forgiveness was clumsily beheaded by six blows of the axe.

The recriminations that followed Monmouth's misguided uprising against the Catholic King were so brutal that their memory has become part of West Country folklore. Judge Jeffreys – 'he'll rip yer guts out and show them to you afterwards' – held judgement over the rebels in a cruel and merciless manner. Even spectators of the uprising were condemned to death. In Bristol, typical of those who were executed was Edward Tippet. In his defence, Tippet said he only went to see Monmouth's army. . . 'he never had any aims to wrong any person in life or estate.' Despite his pleas Tippet was hung, along with two other men, on Redcliffe Hill, just outside the south western gate of St Mary Redcliffe. It is told how the simple Tippet could scarcely believe what was happening 'he continued cheerful, not changing his colour to the last moment.' Afterwards his body was drawn and quartered.[13]

Jeffreys, an unpleasant, peevish, and self-righteous character, revelled in his bloodthirsty work. His dark moods were further inflamed by the pain he suffered from gallstones. In order to relieve his discomfort he drank heavily. Bristol was the last stop of Jeffrey's tour of the West Country and he lost no time in revealing his abrupt character. At an official reception on September 22nd, Jeffreys was soon lashing out threats that had even the councillors shaking in their seats. His forceful monologue, full of venom and anger, gives a chilling impression of the Judge's mood. He gave the councillors a 'lick with the rough side of his tongue' as he put it. He scoffed at the splendours of his reception and declared that he had not come to make set speeches but to do the 'business of a gracious King.' Jeffreys continued with a torrent of attacks on the city; he jeered at the influence women were supposed to have over civic affairs and then burst into a denunciation of the execution of Charles I whom he claimed was the 'most blessed martyr after Jesus.' As to his task of punishing Monmouth's rebels, he asserted that rebellion 'is like the sin of witchcraft' and implied that the city was brimming over with rebels: 'Gentlemen, I must tell you, I am afraid that this city has too many of these people (rebels) in it, and it is your duty to search them out . . . I have brought a brush in my pocket and I shall be sure to rub the dirt wherever it lies, on whomsoever it sticks. Gentlemen, I shall not stand complementing with you: I shall talk with some of you before I part.' In conclusion to his speech, the Judge not only censured the magistrates for being corrupt in their dispensation of justice but also rounded on the Mayor and accused him of being a 'kidnapping knave,' whom he would have hanged there and then had it not been for his respect of the city.[14]

Despite these threats only six people were condemned for high treason in Bristol: a small number in comparison to the hundreds he had executed elsewhere. The assize was a vivid warning of how perilous it was to contest the authority of the King. Even so, only three years after this pitchfork rebellion, William of Orange, a devout Protestant, was able to engineer a successful and bloodless insurrection, the Glorious Revolution of 1688. This time, in a remarkable fit of hysteria and nosebleeds, James II panicked and fled the country vacating the throne for the Dutch William and his wife Mary (James II's daughter).

Judge Jeffreys died three months later in the Tower of London – of natural causes.

LESS ADMIRABLE VENTURES

From the middle of the seventeenth century, new exotic imports such as tobacco, sugar and rum – products that were soon to become inextricably connected with Bristol's prosperity were increasingly to be seen unloaded at the dockside.

Since the end of the Civil War, Bristolians had been able to concentrate on matters closer to their hearts – their trade and industry. At last Bristol was emerging from its economic doldrums. The 1650s was a time of economic growth; a growth particularly encouraged by a Parliament keen to see the expansion of the colonial trade – especially if it was carried in English ships. This Parliamentary support of trade, combined with the hardworking Puritan outlook and the increased contact with the New World seemed to provide an infallible recipe for Bristol's success.

After almost two centuries Cabot's discovery was proving its worth with opportunities in both North America and the West Indies being exploited. Although the traditional Irish, Spanish and Portuguese trades were still of considerable importance it was the trade with the West Indies, Virginia and Newfoundland that brought in real riches. Merchants were able to prosper whichever way they turned as there were good profits to be made on both outward and inward journeys. Exports included cloth, groceries, cheese, bacon, nails, iron, glass and soap – in fact all those commodities that were needed to sustain the new colonies. On the homeward journey, further dividends could be made by returning via the Iberian Peninsula and exchanging fish for oil, wine and fruit.

This is not to say that those involved did not take risks: there were the ever-present dangers from pirates, navigational error and shipwreck. Also tobacco and sugar cargoes were especially vulnerable to damp and salt water.

There was a darker side to the dawning of Bristol's so-called 'Golden Age.' Initially

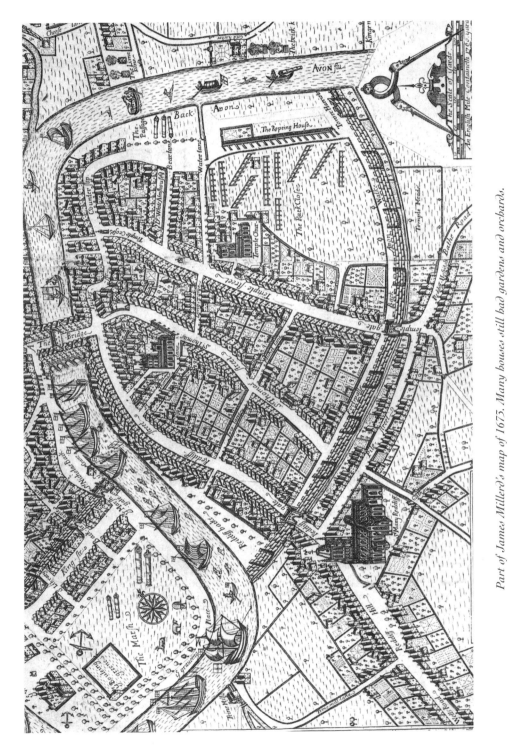

Part of James Millerd's map of 1673. Many houses still had gardens and orchards.
(City of Bristol Museum and Art Gallery).

ships set their sights directly westwards but from the latter part of the seventeenth century the merchants' lust for profit became even more voracious. Ships increasingly sailed south to the African coast to become involved in less admirable ventures.

In the opening years of the seventeenth century it had been the proud boast of Englishmen that, whatever other countries did, they abhorred the trade in human flesh. But with the demands for labour in the new colonies and the Eastern American seaboard these ideals rapidly changed. Greed overcame morality. For the outwardly respectable merchants, out of sight was out of mind; their lust for money defeated their scruples. Many years later in 1765, John Pinney, a member of the famous Bristol merchant family, wrote about a visit to the West Indies that he was 'shocked at the first appearance of human flesh for sale.' But he reasoned that 'surely God ordained them for the use and benefit of us, otherwise his Divine Will would have made some particular sign or token'[15].

In the early days of the slave trade, London had been granted a royal charter which specifically excluded all other ports from participating in this lucrative enterprise. But with such high stakes on offer Bristolians were unwilling to sit back on the sidelines. Small numbers traded with the African coast regardless. The trade was eventually authorised for Bristolians in 1698 and by 1725 it has been calculated that Bristol's ships were carrying yearly 17,000 slaves to the new world. Again, there were risks – for sailors it was a notoriously dangerous and pest-ridden journey – estimates indicate that perhaps 25 per cent of sailors leaving for the Golden Triangle would not return. Not for nothing did they sing:

> *Beware and take care of the Bight of Benin*
> *There's one that comes out for forty went in.*

So from the middle of the seventeenth century onwards it must always be borne in mind that Bristol's riches, directly or indirectly, came from slavery. Indeed, it was only in the last decade of the twentieth century that Bristol officially started to face up to this fact. The milestone exhibition *A Respectable Trade?* mounted by the Bristol City Museums and Art Gallery in 1999 demolished many myths and presented the full facts about slavery in a clear, concise and unambiguous way. It reinforced the fact that transported Africans and their enforced contribution to the production of tobacco, sugar and rum were the cornerstone of Bristol's great wealth in the eighteenth century.

EDWARD COLSTON

In present day Bristol, Edward Colston is a name one cannot ignore. There are Colston Streets and Colston Roads, there are Colston Schools, there is a Colston Hall and there

*Bristol's famous philanthropist Edward Colston (1636-1721) took an active part
in the planning and financing of slaving ventures to West Africa.
Bust by Rysbrack. (City of Bristol Museum and Art Gallery)*

is even a Colston Bun. Colston's name is everywhere. But what do we actually know about the man himself?

Edward Colston, the eldest child of William Colston, a wealthy merchant of Wine Street was born in Temple Street in 1636. Initially, Colston made his money through a varied trade with Spain and other Mediterranean countries. His luck as a merchant was notorious – 'he never insured a ship and he never lost one.'[16] Even so, for many years a mystery surrounded his wealth. It was naively remarked by the eighteenth century historian William Barrett that 'there has never yet been given any account how his fortune accumulated so fast.'[17]

Colston's true character is shielded by an armour of apocryphal tales. When asked why he never married, he is supposed to have retorted that 'every helpless widow is my wife and every distressed orphan is my child.' Then there is the fascinating tale of the dolphin that rescued one of Colston's ships by pressing its body against the holed vessel thereby plugging a leak. Colston is also credited with bringing the first pineapples to Britain.

Stories aside, there can be no doubt that Colston was a generous benefactor to the city of his birth. He was always keen to remember his roots and among the many charities that he supported he took a particular interest in the affairs of his native parish, founding a charity school in Temple Street and granting money to Temple Church. Even so, despite his benevolent gifts, his relationship with the City Corporation was often strained. Colston was a man of strong convictions; he was a dedicated Tory and a vehement hater of the Roman Catholic Church. When James II passed the Declaration of Indulgence in 1687 Colston felt that the Bristol Corporation was veering dangerously towards Catholicism and dissent.

Although for all practical purposes he was a Londoner – he had been living in London since he was eighteen – it is suggested that because of these threatened changes he sold his Bristol ships and closed down his local transactions.

By 1689 Colston had settled permanently in a modest mansion in Mortlake in Surrey. Here, among a number of servants, he had a black maid and grew oranges in the garden. He nevertheless continued to dispatch his benevolent gifts to Bristol – though only infrequently did he visit the city himself.

His charities did, however, have strings attached to them. At Temple School, children of Catholics or dissenters were not admitted while books containing any 'tincture of whiggism' were forbidden. On one occasion, Colston wrote to the governors of Temple School to denounce the energetic vicar of the parish, Arthur Bedford, claiming that his conduct was a scandal and that he was not a true son of the church. In Colston's view Bedford's low church beliefs were as obnoxious as anything preached by nonconformists.[18]

Over the following years such dogmatism was excused of a man who otherwise had such a generous reputation. Indeed on Colston's death several Colston Societies sprang up 'to keep his memory green.' And these societies performed their task well, for by the late Victorian era the esteem in which Colston was held had grown to such an extent that he seemed almost ripe for canonisation. In fact, Nichols and Taylor (Taylor was president in 1840 of the Colston-inspired Dolphin Society) whimsically wrote of Colston in their otherwise useful history of Bristol that 'the grand old man passed, on the 22nd October 1721, into the presence of his Lord, to be greeted with the words "well done, good and faithful servant."[19]

But how had Colston made his money? It was only in the 1920s that the Colston myth came to be reassessed. At that time, a speaker to the Colston Society jokingly chided his audience by adding, when he toasted their patron 'of whom you know absolutely next to nothing.'[20] The speaker was right, for the benefactions of Colston are well known but the character of the man and his source of wealth continue to be clouded by mystery.

Colston's secret had remained well hidden, or ignored, for a long time. But subsequent research revealed that the bulk of his wealth came, of course, from his close involvement with the slave trade. In 1680 Edward Colston became a member of the Royal African Company and took an active part in the planning and financing of slaving ventures to East Africa, his name appearing in the company records for the following eleven years.

The paradox is that whilst Colston was closely involved with the slave trade he was undoubtedly a charitable and religious man. Even so, it is fitting that Colston's statue in the Centre of Bristol depicts him with his head bowed – bowed with humility or with shame? Yet Colston should not be the only merchant singled out for this dual morality. There were many other people whose hands were also soiled by the dirty money of the slave trade.

Notes
1. T. R. Robinson, *Sieges of Bristol During the Civil War* (Oxford, 1861) p.31
2. Richard Atkyns, *Military Memoirs of the Civil War* (ed. Peter Young) p. 28
3. P. McGrath, *Bristol and the Civil War* (1981) p.46
4. S. Seyer, *Memoirs of Bristol* (Bristol, 1822-1825) Vol 11, p.452
5. P. McGrath, op cit, p.42
6. S. Seyer, op cit p.461
7. ibid p.458-459
8. A. CliftonTaylor, *English Parish Churches as Works of Art*, p.160
9. S. Seyer, op cit, p.483496
10. Russell Mortimer, *Early Bristol Quakers* (Bristol, 1967) p.4
11. S. Seyer, op cit, p.509
12. Samuel Pepys diary, August 1st, 1667.
13. J. Evans, *A Chronological Outline of the History of Bristol* (1824) p.240
14. J.F. Nichols and J. Taylor, *Bristol Past and Present* (1881) Vol 3, p.112-113
15. C. M. Maclnnes, *Bristol and the Slave Trade in Bristol in the 18th Century* (ed. P. McGrath, 1972) p.117
16. W. Barrett, *The History and the Antiquities of Bristol* (Bristol, 1789) p.655
17. ibid p. 655
18. J. Latimer *Annals of 18th Century Bristol* (Bristol, 1893) p.86
19. J. F. Nichols and J. Taylor, op cit, p.136
20. H. J. Wilkins, *Edward Colston* (Bristol, 1920) p.4

Other Sources
P. Fryer, *Staying Power, The History of Black People in Britain* (London, 1984). R. Mortimer, *Minute Book of the Men's Meeting of the Society of Friends in Bristol 1686-1704* (Bristol Record Society, Bristol, 1977). B. Little, *City and County of Bristol* (1954). C. M. Maclnnes, *Bristol: A Gateway to the Empire* (1968). Bristol Broadsides, *Bristol's Other History* (1983). Bristol Museums and Art Gallery *Slave Trade Trail* (1998)

Neptune, Bristol's most travelled statue. Here, in 1825,
standing by the conduit at the corner of Bear Lane.
(City of Bristol Museum and Art Gallery)

FOUR

THE GOLDEN AGE

The beginning of the eighteenth century saw Bristol entering its 'Golden Age,' an exciting pioneering era when trade and industry expanded at an unprecedented rate.

Although domesticated animals still freely roamed the streets, the Southern Parishes had lost their spacious rural character. Daniel Defoe wrote of Bristol in 1723 'that there is hardly room to set another house in it.' Bristol was now a bustling, frontier town, the streets echoing with exciting news and rumour from the new colonies and other far off places.

Visiting Londoners, however, accustomed to the wide streets and the new styles of architecture that had grown out of the ashes of the Great Fire of 1666, were often surprised by Bristol's old fashioned and grimy appearance. As Bristol had been through no such cleansing process as the Fire the impression of the city, which was constructed in a half timbered style more befitting the fifteenth century, was distinctly provincial. To Londoners it all seemed very out of date. When Horace Walpole visited Bristol in 1766 he remained unimpressed by all the industriousness around him and merely remarked that Bristol was 'the dirtiest great shop I ever saw.'[1]

Daniel Defoe was equally scathing in *A Tour thro' the whole island of Great Britain*, the first comprehensive, and regularly updated, guide book of Britain. In his first edition, published in 1723, he was particularly unflattering about Bristol and its inhabitants:

'The greatest inconveniences of Bristol are its situation, its narrow streets and the narrowness of its river...'

Adding insult to injury Defoe continued:

'and we might mention also another narrow that is the mind of the generality of the people; for let me tell you, the merchants of Bristol, tho' very rich are not like the merchants of London...'

Defoe did, however, seem to approve of Bristol's puritanical streak:

'A great face of seriousness and religion appears in Bristol. and the magistrates are

53

laudably strict in exacting the observation of the sabbath, considering the general dissoluteness that has broken out almost everywhere else.'

Alexander Pope on his visit in 1739 was also most unimpressed:

'The city itself is very unpleasant with no civilised company in it...the streets were as crowded as London, but the best image I can give you of it is 'Tis as if Wapping and Southwark were ten times as big; or all their people ran into London.' [2]

But despite these adverse comments, Bristol was nationally famous for its maritime trade, and the parishes of Redcliffe, Temple and St Thomas known for their industries. These ranged in size from small backroom enterprises to larger concerns of national repute. Many of the industries relied on coal from Kingswood in their production; consequently some made a considerable impact on the environment. Indeed, Alexander Pope commented that his first impression of Bristol was of a city overshadowed by 'twenty odd pyramids smoking over the town.'[3] These tall brick cones, necessary for the production of glass and pottery, were beginning to compete with the church towers and spires for the dominance of Bristol's skyline. The tall glass houses not only changed the skyline of Bristol but also, together with the fumes from the soap makers, the tallow chandlers and the sugar boilers, polluted with smoke and 'noxious effluvia' the atmosphere of the Avon valley – especially so during calm anti-cyclonic weather. To make conditions even more unpleasant during the day, there was a constant barrage of noise from the numerous coopers, smiths and braziers in the parishes.

Of course, many people were employed in the Southern Parishes in the provision and maintenance of Bristol's expanding fleet. There were shipbuilders, sail, chain and rope makers and numerous coopers providing the kegs and barrels that were indispensable for long journeys. And in conjunction with the unusual and exotic commodities arriving at the quayside there was a new breed of industry – tobacco rolling, tobacco cutting, pipemaking and sugar refining – that indicated a widening and changing world. All in all, the Southern Parishes of Bristol had become an area as industrialised as anywhere else in the country at the time. `Commerce might be king in Bristol' wrote Patrick McGrath, `but in industry it found a worthwhile consort.'[4]

SUGAR

Of all the new enterprises, sugar refining was one of the most important. Whilst the wealth of Bristol's new up-and-coming rival, Liverpool, was said to have derived from slaves and cotton, Bristol's eighteenth century riches have been attributed to slaves

View of South Bristol in 1717. 'The city itself' wrote Alexander Pope in 1739 'is very unpleasant with no civilised company in it.'
(City of Bristol Museum and Art Gallery)

and sugar. The sugar refining industry which was carried out on a large scale was, however, disliked by many parishioners because it created both fumes and a fire risk. The raw sugar, which was boiled in large copper vats, was heated to such a high temperature that it was prone to ignite – something not to be encouraged in a city whose dwellings were built mostly of wood and in an age when the most sophisticated piece of firefighting equipment was a bucket.

Indeed in 1661 there were so many complaints regarding John Hine's sugar house in Thomas Street that he was forced to close and move to less crowded quarters off Temple Street 'where he could give no further offense.'[5] However, in 1661, what had been feared for so long happened: a sugar house in Redcliffe caught fire one night and burnt to the ground causing £1,000 worth of damage. Worse was to come the following year when another refinery in the same street burst into flames on a dark and blustery night. The strong winds fanned the fire which soon threatened widespread destruction. At first, there was chaos. No buckets could be found for water and to make matters even more difficult those people hunting for water containers could not see, for their candles were blown out by the wind. Eventually when the buckets were located they were found to be riddled with holes. It was more by luck than anything else that the fire spread no further. The Corporation must have learnt one small lesson for not long afterwards it was proposed that they keep a store of torches for times when candles were unsuitable.

The refining of sugar obviously had its problems, but it was a lucrative business and was to remain a staple industry of the Southern Parishes for many years.

CROWN, FLINT AND BOTTLE GLASS

The rise of the glass industry in the city was remarkably rapid. In the earlier part of the seventeenth century the majority of glass makers in the country were located in the Weald of Sussex. The rapid demise of the Sussex industry was brought about by an acute shortage of fuel. The glass makers and iron founders of the Weald had denuded the landscape of timber to such an extent that legislation had to be passed in 1615 forbidding the use of 'Timber or Wood, or any Fewell made of Timber or Wood,'[6] in their manufacturing processes. In effect the new law put an end to the Sussex glass industry.

This scarcity of wood, and the ensuing legislation, together with the discovery of a method for making glass using coal, enabled Bristol to become a natural successor to the Weald. Bristol not only had coal deposits on its doorstep at Kingswood, it also had sand and limestone at hand. Redcliffe sand, tunnelled from the caves or dug straight from the ground was particularly suitable for thick bottle glass.

A whole range of glass was soon being produced – there were makers of decorative glass, window glass and most numerous of all, bottle makers. Bottles were particularly in demand for the storage of both imported wine and locally produced cider and perry, some of which went to the West Indies.

To enable coal to generate a temperature high enough to produce glass, towering brick cones were built to increase the draught needed to fire the furnaces. As contemporary views show, these cones were large structures, some being up to 90 feet high and 50 feet in diameter round the base. Millerd's map of Bristol in 1710 shows six glasshouses in the city, five of these being in the Southern Parishes. The cones were expensive to build and indeed were sometimes not constructed to the highest specifications. It was reported that:

'A large glass house belonging to Sir Abraham Elton Bart...suddenly fell down; happy it was for the glassmen that the fire was out...' [7]

Once the cone was built, however, the production of glass was inexpensive. The glass maker's art lay more in his skill than his tools, his equipment consisted merely of a blowing iron, a few wooden implements for shaping and sometimes a mould for blowing glass into.

The process was observed by a man who simply called himself the 'Irish Gentleman' and wrote:

'I saw many glass houses, with which this town vastly abounds, as the inhabitants reckon upwards of thirty. The generality of them are built of brick, toperwise to the top. Within side is the Chaldron wherein the metal is boiled, by means of a large constant fire with a chimney, by which the smoke is conveyed to the top...I saw several things blown, this is performed by a long iron tube, the end of which they dip into the metal, and after they have given it a blast or two they form or shape it on an anvil.' [8]

The Irish Gentleman was not alone in being fascinated by the production of glass. Many visitors to the city, along with day trippers from the spa town of Bath, made a specific detour to observe this fascinating industry. By the end of the eighteenth century it was such a popular sight that *Mathews' Bristol Directory* recommended that:

'They who are strangers to the working of window glass, and to the blowing of white or flint glass which is formed in such a variety of modes and forms, may gratify their curiosity of observing these curious operations by presenting a small gratuity to the workmen, who living in hot climates are very glad of some suction to moisten their clay.'

Although the demand for glass from the new colonies and home was usually stable, the market was sometimes upset by outside influences. The excise tax imposed in 1696 of one shilling on twelve bottles hit the industry particularly hard. As a consequence of the duty many people found it cheaper to put their liquor in casks. Between this date and 1710 it seems that three of the nine glass houses in the city closed down.

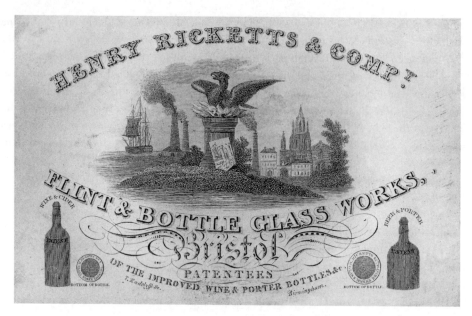

Billhead for Henry Ricket's glass works. In the late eighteenth century the Southern Parishes became an important national centre for the production of glass.
(City of Bristol Museum and Art Gallery)

Tile picture, dated 1820, of the Bristol Pottery on Temple Back.
(City of Bristol Museum and Art Gallery)

Nevertheless there were soon signs of the industry's recovery. In the next ten years four new glasshouses opened. Demand was further stimulated by the popularity of the Hotwell Spa. There was an extensive trade in bottles for the sale of Hotwell Water which was marketed in London for the exhorbitant price of six shillings for a dozen of the largest bottles.

Today, apart from the world famous antique Bristol Blue glass and other highly prized Bristol glass objects, little is left to remind us of this once thriving industry. Except, that is, the truncated remains of Bristol's last glass cone which has been incorporated into the buildings of the Jarvis Hotel on Redcliffe Way. The cone of Messrs H. & T. Proctor stayed intact until the 1930s when weaknesses in the upper brickwork of the glasshouse meant that it needed to be cut down to its present 25 feet height. Once more the chink of glass can be heard in this industrial monument – the chink of wine glasses, for the cone now houses the hotel's restaurant.

SAUCEBOATS AND GALLEYPOTS

The numerous brick cones that pierced Bristol's skyline were not exclusively associated with glassworks – some housed potteries. Around the middle of the eighteenth century great advances were made in ceramic technology. At a time when virtually everybody ate from pewter plates, or more usually wooden trenchers, it was every potter's dream to be able to produce the high quality porcelain that was so expensively imported from China. As no source in England was yet known for kaolin, a whole variety of pastes and glazes were used as experimental alternatives. In late sixteenth century Bristol the nearest the potters could get to producing a ceramic look-alike was delftware. The making of delftware, named after the Dutch town where the technique was perfected, involved dipping and sealing the already fired earthenware 'biscuit' into an opaque lead glaze.

The oldest pottery in the Bristol area to make delftware was the Galleypot Manufactory in the village of Brislington. In 1684 the Brislington Pottery moved to premises on Temple Back. What is remarkable about the Brislington Pottery is that it continued in production, under one name or another, until the 1960s. The Pountney Bristol Pottery, as it was then known, moved from its premises in Temple Back to St Philips in 1884 and then to its final site at Lodge Causeway in 1906; it closed down in 1968 when it was the last surviving link with a tradition of industrial pottery that extended back to the Middle Ages.

By the mid 1740s, experiments in England in the manufacture of something that resembled porcelain were more successful. Strange mixtures of bone ash, glass frit, soapstone and so on were being used in the creation of what was called 'Soft Paste' porcelain. The production of this most sought after white ware involved difficult, secret and expensive manufacturing processes. Even so, the partnership of two Quakers, Benjamin Lund and William Miller, who established a factory on Redcliffe Back in 1750, was able to advertise for sale 'Very beautiful white sauce boats.' The quality of these sauceboats so impressed a group of businessmen from the West Midlands that they approached Lund to help them with the difficulties they were experiencing in their own manufactory. In 1752 Lund left Redcliffe and transferred all his stocks, utensils and equipment to the establishment that was one day to become the famous Worcester Porcelain Company.

Eventually, in 1765, another Quaker, William Cooksworthy, discovered a source of kaolin in Cornwall allowing true hardpaste porcelain to be manufactured in England for the first time. Cooksworthy, a Plymouth chemist, moved his works to Castle Green in Bristol and by 1770, to the envy of his rivals, was producing true Bristol Porcelain.

Yet despite the quest for porcelain one must not forget that the bulk of Bristol's pottery output was of a less glamorous, more utilitarian nature. All the potteries also made ordinary household ware, demand for which was more stable and less dependent on the fashion of the day. The majority produced 'redware' – bricks, pantiles, chimney pots, drainpipes and sugar moulds – whilst Frank's Pottery on Redcliffe Back specialised in stoneware, glaze on the inside only, which was particularly suitable for jars and pots, which they made in all shapes and sizes.

SOAP

Any description of the industries of the Southern Parishes would be incomplete without mentioning the humble, and sometimes not so humble, soapmakers. Soap was initially introduced to serve the woollen industry. For many centuries Bristol had enjoyed a great reputation for its soap, and in the twelfth century was so famous for this industry that Richard of Devizes had satirically suggested that soapmaking was the mainstay of Bristol's wealth. Even though this was an exaggeration, soapmaking was carried out on a large scale and much money could be made from it. Such a fortune was acquired in the later years of Elizabeth's reign by Alderman Robert Rogers who lived in the Great House, just off Bristol Bridge at the top end of Redcliffe Street. This house was so sumptuous that when Samuel Pepys saw it he described it as 'if fit for a King's palace.'

In 1633, the Bristol Soapmakers felt it necessary to prove the superior quality of their product in comparison to that produced by the Society of Soapmakers of Westminster. Accordingly Captain Conningsby organised a demonstration where two women washed some napkins, one using Westminster soap, the other Bristol soap. The result was as hoped for…

'It did appear and it was soe confessed by the said captaine Conningsby that the said Bristoll sope was as good in all respects as the saide sope by him produced. And allthough the saide napkins washed with Bristoll soape weare alltogether, as white washed and sweet or rather sweter than the other yet in the washing of the saide napkins there was not alltogether soe much soap expended of the saide Bristoll soape as there was of the other soape. Soe it appeared to all present, that the saide Bristoll soape was as good or rather better than the saide other soape.' [9]

In short, in the timeless words of the soap commercial: 'Bristol soap washes whiter.'

A NEW ECONOMIC FORCE

If there is one group that stands out in the eighteenth century for their prodigious commercial and financial acumen it is the Quakers. A characteristic of Bristol's eighteenth century industries is the number of enterprises, particularly capital-intensive ones, that were run by Friends. At a time when no banks were available (the first Bristol bank was established in 1750 – and then it was the only bank in the country outside London) the willingness of Quakers to join together in the sponsorship of enterprises created a new economic force in the city. For the first time the establishment of new ventures was not left solely in the hands of the very rich.

Although the Friends were hardworking and scrupulously honest they nevertheless had a long struggle to gain respectability within the establishment. And even though the Friends had lost the fiery fanaticism that so characterised the early days of Quakerism they were still viewed as targets for discrimination; even in 1711 The Merchants Society ruled that no member should be a Quaker.

Matters were made particularly difficult for the Quakers in the years after the Restoration of the monarchy. Because of their refusal to swear the compulsory oath of allegiance to the crown – Quakers would only obey God, not men – they were branded as traitors to the newly established King. In Bristol, this act of defiance was seized upon by the authorities as an excuse for the punishment of Friends in all manner of ways: they were fined, jailed, transported abroad and even threatened with execution.

The most persistent period of persecution was the 1680s. The meeting houses were vandalised and boarded up, sometimes with Friends still in them, and many Quakers were thrown into Newgate Gaol – a place so nasty and stinking that one alderman was heard to say that he wouldn't send his dog to it. In 1684, Robert Vickris, a successful businessman, was sentenced to death, as an example to others for failing to take the oath. Vickris appealed against the sentence, his case being taken to the King's Bench in London and presented to the notorious Judge Jeffreys. In a rare moment of compassion Jeffreys freed the Quaker.

Vickris was lucky; such was the severity of the persecution of Quakers that when the newly crowned James II issued in 1685 his Declaration of Indulgence freeing all dissenters from prosecution over one hundred Quakers were subsequently released from Bristol's Newgate Prison.

Although the Act of Toleration of 1689 gave freedom of rights to dissenters it could not confer upon the Quakers immediate social acceptability. The hectoring of Quakers was to continue, albeit sporadically, for many years. In 1714 there was a degenerate attack on some Quakers during the celebrations for George I's accession. A drunken mob attacked the Temple Street Meeting House as well as some private dwellings. In Tucker Street they broke into the house of a Quaker, Mr Stephens, and refused to leave. When Stephens tried to eject the drunks they became violent and began to ransack his house, forcing open boxes and drawers and plundering plate and other goods. A fellow Quaker who attempted to come to Stephen's rescue was beaten to the ground, kicked about and mortally wounded.

Afterwards the rioters made their way across the river and over to the Custom House causing the ladies, it is reported, to flee in terror from the Coronation Ball. It was not until midnight that the mob dispersed.[10]

The next day, although it was rumoured that the ringleaders had escaped, several of the drunks were rounded up and brought to trial. They were fined £7 together with a prison sentence of three months – a punishment considered by many to be unduly lenient.[11]

TURNPIKE ROADS – THE SPIDER'S WEB

Bristol's rapidly developing commercial and industrial importance depended on its position at the centre of a great regional and coastal trading area. As transport by road was scarcely any the less dirty, dangerous and unreliable than it had been in the Middle Ages most of Bristol's products were transported by sea or river. Nationally the rivers, particularly the Severn and the Mersey, which were reputed to carry more traffic than any other rivers in Europe, remained the arteries of the seventeenth century. River transport did have disadvantages though; safe navigation could frequently be hindered by tidal movements, silting-up and seasonal variations of water depth.

If new markets were to be opened up and trade expanded, those areas away from water transport had to be exploited. From 1706 private trusts were authorised to take on the work of improving roads as the cost was beyond the purse strings of most parishes. These trusts were then permitted to recoup the cost of their outlay by collecting tolls from the road users.

By the end of the eighteenth century the City had outgrown its walls. Redcliffe Gate
was demolished in 1771, Temple Gate in 1808.

For long-distance travellers the new turnpike roads brought about a considerable improvement of conditions. Local people, however, were not always so keen on the changes. Turnpike tolls signified an erosion of an age old liberty – since time immemorial people had travelled the road for free; to many, the very independence of the English way of life was at stake. In fact tolls were to be a cause of riot and strife throughout the eighteenth century and the Southern Parishes were to witness more domestic bloodshed and anger through these impositions than anything else. The English have always disliked road tolls; even one hundred years after their introduction William Cobbett in his *Rural Rides* avoided the turnpikes, as they symbolised the forces that were sublimating the life of the country to that 'great wen,' London, to which the turnpike roads ran like the web of a spider.

In 1749 a new Turnpike Act was introduced and Bristolians quickly found their city surrounded by toll gates. Many of the country people were incensed by the infringement of their rights and in 1749, in an outright act of defiance, several of the toll gates outside the city were destroyed. The Turnpike Commissioners were not to be that easily discouraged. While new gates were being built they put chains across the roads and continued to collect the hated tolls. This only served to increase the anger of the Somerset folk. An angry crowd of several hundred people chanting 'down with the turnpikes' marched on the city. Some 'naked with only trouzers on', others with their faces blacked for anonymity, presented a fearsome sight as they came over Redcliffe Hill and approached Redcliffe Gate. As both the southern gates of Redcliffe and Temple were closed the crowd turned their energies to demolishing the Totterdown toll gate. They were soon pursued by a retaliatory force of police officers and constables, several turnpike commissioners and a rough bunch of sailors armed with muskets, pistols and cutlasses. After a brief but violent skirmish at the Totterdown toll gate the protesters dispersed.

But this was not the end of the disturbances; a magistrate was accosted and, more ominously, several letters were sent to the Mayor threatening to burn down the city. The threats were taken so seriously that a state of alert was declared. Troops were called in, the city gates were closed at 10.00pm every night and notice was given to the citizens that they should be prepared to defend Bristol from further attack.[12]

In fact, the intimidation came to nothing and calm was soon restored. A couple of days later the *Bristol Journal* was pleased to report that 'all those wounded in the Totterdown Conflict are in a fair way of recovery except Farmer Barnes, and even of him there are hopes.'[13]

These localised protests went largely unheeded and the turnpike trusts slowly spread their web of roads across the country. The effect of the new road system was far-reaching and often unforeseen. The turnpikes necessitated not only a new approach to road making but also stimulated innovations in the design of vehicles.

In 1747 a slow moving wagon left Thomas Street every Friday completing its eighty mile trip to Exeter by the following Tuesday.[14] With the introduction of coaches, conditions improved so much that by 1765 the coach leaving in the morning from The George in Temple Street arrived in Exeter the following day.[15] The cost for this speedy trip was one guinea. As methods of long distance travel were revolutionised (to make the ride a little less bumpy, harsh metal springs were increasingly substituted by soft leather straps) excursions turned from uncomfortable adventures into experiences that could almost be pleasurable.

By 1784 communication with London had improved to such an extent that a novel sight, the Royal Mail coach, was to be seen crossing Bristol Bridge and making its way as briskly as possible down Temple Street to the Bath Road. These new speedy coaches, delivering letters to the capital in just one day, were protected by guards, the cost of which was defrayed by passengers who also wanted to benefit from the increased speed and security. Only four passengers were carried by the two horse coach and the fare for this exhilarating journey was £1 8s 0d.[16] There was one drawback, however, this being the common belief that the speed attained by these coaches was dangerous to health. Travellers were warned to take care on these journeys for people had been known to 'die of apoplexy from the rapidity of the motion.' In winter, hypothermia was a more likely hazard.

In Bristol, the increase in vehicles on the roads caused jams at bottlenecks created by the gateways and Bristol Bridge. Even before the coaching revolution, Daniel Defoe had complained about Bristol's narrow streets. Particularly hazardous to both pedestrians and passengers were the city gates and the overcrowded bridge. Both became quickly congested by the constant flow of 'seamen, women, children, loaded horses, asses and sledges' and were a frequent source of frustration and complaint. Accidents such as a man having 'his leg broke on the Bridge by the Wheel of a waggon going over it' were common.[18]

The narrow bridge was made especially hazardous by its incline towards the centre which caused passing high loads to lock.[19] These problems, backed up by the occasional petition of complaint, indicated that matters would soon have to be rectified. And, besides, the bridge was distinctly unfashionable and hardly befitted the status of the Kingdom's second city. The medieval London Bridge had long been replaced by a new model of elegant simplicity.

Two options were available; either the original bridge could be retained and widened or it could be replaced by a totally new structure. Whatever course was taken the cost would be enormous; not only would it include the demolition of some thirty houses that were perched upon the old structure but also the consequent loss of revenue from this property. A committee of twenty-four members was set up, and decided that a new, one arch bridge should be built, adjoined by a temporary structure whilst work was in progress. But when the committee's proposals were presented to the Council they were quickly rejected in preference of the cheaper solution of widening. To the chagrin of the city's merchants the committee also suggested that the cost of these improvements could be covered by a duty on coal, a rate on houses, a wharfage charge on imports and exports

West end of Redcliffe Parade – a speculative building project financed through money made by privateering
(City of Bristol Museum and Art Gallery)

together with a toll on the bridge for five years. Such an uproar ensued between the bridge committee, the councillors and the merchants that the entire scheme was shelved.

An independent group of businessmen took the opportunity of the stalemate to present a private bill to Parliament authorising its promoters to carry out the proposed construction. The threat of a private venture taking over Bristol's one and only bridge across the Avon gave the Council the vital impetus to resume their proceedings. Even though the Council now backed the proposals for a new bridge rather than a widened one, further controversy raged over the design of the structure. After a phenomenal seventy six meetings it was finally decided to build a bridge of three arches on the original piers designed by John Bridges (and inspired by Westminster Bridge – though it is difficult to recognise this now, due to Victorian widening).

The new bridge, eventually financed as suggested (but omitting the duty on coal), was opened for foot passengers in 1768 and for traffic in 1769.

It wasn't only the bridge that became congested with traffic; if there was to be a free flow of vehicles through Redcliffe, Temple and St Thomas further modifications were needed. The city gates were an obvious problem, yet many councillors were loath to demolish them for security reasons. The city gates were important for regulating the flow of strangers into the city. In 1674 both Redcliffe and Temple Gates were manned at night by five watchmen who were to look out for foreigners. In 1730 a petition from the Temple parishioners claimed that the gates were 'incommodious and dangerous.' After further protests from Redcliffe residents £250 was spent on replacing the medieval gates with a new structure in a dubiously named 'rustic classic style.' In 1734 Temple Gate was also rebuilt.[20] Yet the new gates offered little improvement; for although side passages were now provided for pedestrians the width of the roadway for carriages was still restricted. Soon pleas for demolition were heard again.

The character of the city was changing rapidly. One only had to stand at Redcliffe Gate and look southward – where there had previously been countryside there were now houses. There were new buildings on Redcliffe Hill and along the Addercliffe, a new speculative building project – the construction of Redcliffe Parade – was being financed by the profits of Sydenham Teast's privateering ventures. There was no escaping the fact that Bristol, like London which in a symbolic and practical act had taken down its gates in 1761, had outgrown its walls. Indeed, even back in 1674 several doorways had been cut illegally into the Redcliffe and Temple walls to make access easier to the fields and gardens in the suburbs. The idea of a walled city in eighteenth century England was an anachronism.

The gates were used for defence so infrequently – the last time being for the Turnpike Riot of 1749 – that there was little justification for their continued presence. Accordingly, the Corporation overcame its conservative instincts and in June 1771 ordered that the new Redcliffe Gate, which was barely 40 years old, be taken down. Temple Gate stayed a little longer. It was in 1808 that a local journal announced the auction of 'material of Temple Gate, now standing at the top of Temple Street.' The materials were bought for £107.

THE MODERN BRIDGE.

The new Bristol Bridge. Inspired by Westminster Bridge, the bridge was opened for foot passengers in 1768, and traffic in 1769.

NUTRITIOUS ALE

As the population of Bristol doubled between 1700 and 1750, so the number of alehouses increased correspondingly. By 1754, with one house in ten in Bristol being an ale house, there were in all 625 in the city. *Sketchley's Bristol Directory* of 1775 lists numerous victuallers – the names of some of their hostelries still being with us today. Familiar establishments are The Ship in the Cathay, The Ostrich in Guinea Street and The (Blue) Bell in Prewitt Street.

Ale figured largely in everybody's diet. The general belief was that the drinking of water, apart from spa water, was to be avoided at all costs. Water, even uncontaminated water, was usually viewed as medically unsound 'being cold, slow and slack of digestion.' Not only was ale safer to drink than water, it was also more nutritious. It has been calculated that one fifth of the nation's dietary requirements were supplied merely through the consumption of ale. During this time a staggering 800 pints per head of population were consumed yearly. The importance of ale was graphically illustrated in Hogarth's engravings of Gin Lane and Beer Street. In the 1730s and 1740s the noticeable rise in the death rate is put down to the high consumption of cheap, nutritiously worthless gin. In 1750, the year before its sale was effectively outlawed, the annual consumption of gin was eight pints per head.[21]

The day started early but then so did the drinking. By 7.00am business was in full swing. Soon, as Defoe found 'just as in London, the taverns and coffee houses were crowded with bargainers and "Bristol Milk", which is Spanish sherry, nowhere as good as here plentifully drunk.'

The finish of work at 6.00pm would normally be followed by drinking in the local tavern. As the only available artificial light was from smoky tallow candles, the fall of dusk signified the time for people to return home and retire to bed.

The consumption of ale was also an every day anaesthetic that made life bearable. Indeed, Dr Johnson (himself a 'hardened and shameless tea drinker...whose kettle has scarcely time to cool') asserted that all decent people of his home town Lichfield got drunk every night and were not thought the worse for it.

Very little excuse was needed for the copious consumption of alcohol. One rather bizarre cause of revelry was the annual perambulation of the city boundaries and the accompanying duck hunt. One day in autumn, members of the council, heralded by the bells of St Mary Redcliffe, would grandly proceed to Treen Mills (now the site of Bathurst Basin), where they would be greeted by the city's trumpeters. When everyone was assembled the ducks would be released onto the mill pond and then, to the delight of all, trained dogs would be set upon them. In 1742, the last recorded Duck Hunt, nineteen birds were purchased for this brutal entertainment. Excessive drinking accompanied the event which culminated in a rowdy walk along the city's boundary with some of the more drunken spectators being tossed up and down on the marking stones. Despite the almost universal penchant for alcohol, there was still an influential class of puritans who looked upon such ribald occasions as sinful and campaigned for their prohibition.

REDCLIFFE'S MOST FAMOUS SON

Thomas Chatterton, Redcliffe's most famous son, was born in the shadow of Redcliffe Church in 1752. He became 'the boy wonder' who wrote poetry that was to be admired for many generations. Today, his literary achievements are not to everybody's taste. By modern standards his work is often criticised as being too contrived, but even so there is still an honourable place for him in English literature. The story of his life is of a frustrated talent ending in a tragedy truly in keeping with the tenor of his Gothic verse.

Thomas Chatterton was born the posthumous son of a school teacher who was also part-time lay clerk at St Mary Redcliffe. His father died three months before his birth. Within a short time Chatterton's mother moved from the school house into lodgings on Redcliffe Hill where she eked out a living from dressmaking. When her husband was alive she had apparently pilfered some old parchment manuscripts from St Mary Redcliffe for use as patterns. The story goes that the young Chatterton, who at the age of five had been dismissed from school for being too dull to be taught, saw some of these coloured manuscripts and became so engrossed in their beauty that they gave him the vital encouragement to learn to read.

At the age of seven, it was again decided that he should try a formal education and this time he was sent to Colston's School. But once again he found the methods of teaching uninspiring and soon became bored. Yet outside school his thirst for knowledge continued. Within a couple of years he was using the small amounts of pocket-money that his widowed mother could afford to borrow books from a circulating library.

Chatterton left school at fifteen and took up employment as a clerk to an attorney in Corn Street. He worked the usual long hours – 8.00 am to 8.00 pm – and was required to 'live in.' He was so efficient at his job that he found he could often condense his day's work into just a couple of hours. This left him plenty of time to continue with his studies and writing. He read widely, researching into books on the classics, the sciences, music, medicine and history.

About this time a variety of historical manuscripts were discovered by Chatterton. The first of these historical discoveries to be published was an ancient account of the Mayor of Bristol crossing the original newly erected Bristol Bridge in 1248. Chatterton claimed that his report was taken from a medieval manuscript. It was a topical subject for the old bridge had just been demolished and replaced by John Bridges' new structure. Other manuscripts followed. By an incredible chance Chatterton was able to supply an acquaintance, Mr Bergum, with a document indicating the great and noble antiquity of

The poet Thomas Chatterton was born in the shadow of St Mary Redcliffe in 1752.
He died at the age of 17 – a phial of arsenic lay by his side
(Tate Gallery)

his family's background. William Barrett was also glad to use some of Chatterton's manuscripts in his *History and Antiquities of the City of Bristol* which he was compiling at the time. Perhaps most remarkable of all was a marvellous series of poems that came to light that were written by Thomas Rowley, a chaplain, apparently, to the great William Canynges.

All these translations and manuscripts were outright fakes. They were simply a product of Chatterton's fertile imagination and extensive learning. What is surprising, however, is that they were accepted so credulously – it was only after Chatterton's death that suspicion was voiced about the majority of this work. Even the slightest critical inspection would have revealed Chatterton's manuscripts for what they were. Several years later, in 1776, Dr Johnson visited Bristol to inspect the Rowley Poems and was left in no doubt that they were written by Chatterton.

Boswell described how he and Dr Johnson visited Barrett and 'saw some of the originals as they were called, which were executed very artificially.' Upon careful inspection of the manuscripts they were quite 'satisfied of the imposture.' Regardless of the fakes Dr Johnson went on to say that 'This is the most incredible young man that has encountered my knowledge: it is wonderful how the whelp has written such things.'[22] Even after this authoritative judgement Barrett was not convinced of their fraudulence. He went ahead with the publication of his *History of Bristol* which included several of Chatterton's creations and became the laughing stock of the city. He was so humiliated that it is said the shame hastened his death in 1789, the same year as the publication of his book.

The limited success of Chatterton's manuscripts was not enough. He realised that if he was to succeed as a poet he would have to find himself a patron and to this end he wrote to the famous dilettante Horace Walpole. Chatterton's letters were well received but his hopes of sponsorship came to nothing. Filled with despair at his apparently dead-end existence Chatterton let it be known that he was contemplating taking his own life. Barrett became so alarmed at Chatterton's despondency that he invited the young poet to his house for a paternal chat. Chatterton opened his heart to Barrett about his frustrations and after much tearful soul searching he promised to put all thoughts of suicide out of his mind.

Many of Chatterton's problems lay in the fact that Bristol was a literary backwater. The city was better known for its commercial achievements rather than its cultural refinements. Any interest in the arts was reserved at this time for the more effete residents along the Avon valley in Bath. Chatterton was to scornfully write of his home town:

> *'Lost of all learning, elegance and sense,*
> *Long had the famous city told her pence.'* [23]

It was obvious to Chatterton that if he was to make his mark on the literary scene he would have to move to London. Accordingly in April 1770 he took the bold step of leaving Redcliffe for a new life in the capital.

Although the letters Chatterton sent home to his mother boasted of his literary achievements and his admiring group of friends, his existence in London was in reality a turn for the worse. He was soon living the clichéd life of a poet wasting away in his garret. In four months he had written articles, mostly satirical, for eleven different journals. This brought in barely enough money to keep him from starving. When he did earn the fairly substantial sum of five guineas for a light hearted musical piece he spent most of the money on a box of presents which he sent to his family. His landlady in Holborn, Mrs Angel, noticed how weak he was becoming. On one occasion she offered him food but he proudly refused, saying that he was not hungry.

The young Chatterton was desperate for a landslide of fame and fortune; his adolescent impetuousness could not wait for it to trickle in. One morning he was found outstretched on his bed; a phial of arsenic was lying on the floor. The young poet had apparently not eaten for several days. Chatterton was given a pauper's burial in a communal grave. He was seventeen years old when he died.

SLAUGHTER ON BRISTOL BRIDGE

As we have already seen, nothing raised the heckles of Bristolians more than the imposition of tolls on roads and bridges. The expected abolition on September 17th, 1793 of the toll on Bristol Bridge was therefore contemplated with great pleasure. The toll was disliked on three counts. Not only had the toll been a burden to individuals but it was also reckoned to be detrimental to the commerce of the city as a whole. Furthermore the toll commissioners were suspected of making an unreasonable profit at everyone else's expense.

So on the day when the toll was due to cease the gates were joyfully pulled down and burnt. Two days later, however, new gates were erected. According to the commissioners the toll was to continue. The commissioners justified their decision by claiming, to the incredulity of many, that money was still owed for construction costs. For a few days general resentment of the toll quietly smouldered until the evening of Saturday, September 28th when a crowd, many of whom were drunk, gathered by the bridge and set about attacking the gates. The magistrates, after pleading vainly with the crowd to disperse, called in the military in order, they hoped, to avoid further trouble. In fact the presence of the Herefordshire Regiment did little to calm matters and after a prolonged period of physical and verbal harassment the troops were ordered to fire a volley into the air. It had its intended effect – and more. The crowd quickly dispersed leaving on the pavement one person dead from musket fire.

Next morning a jeering group appeared at each end of the bridge. At noon, when men were posted to collect tolls there were scenes of angry protest. The mood was becoming

A List of Persons *Killed* and *Wounded*

(At the late RIOTS in BRISTOL respecting the *Bridge Tolls*,)

On the memorable Evening of the 30th of September,

1793,

In Consequence of the FIRE from the MILITARY;

With the VERDICTS returned by the Coroners' Inquests;

AND

Their AGES, Description of their WOUNDS, &c.

A LIST OF THE KILLED.

JOHN ABBOTT, aged 55, Tiler and Plaisterer.—Verdict, Wilful Murder by Person or Persons unknown.

William Aldridge.—Verdict, Wilful Murder by Person or Persons unknown.

James Howell, Parish of St. James, aged 28, Mason.—Verdict, Wilful Murder by Person or Persons unknown.

William Powell, of Castle Precincts, Baker.—Verdict, Wilful Murder by Person or Persons unknown. [The first Verdict returned by the Jury sworn to inquire the Cause of this Gentleman's Death, was "Wilful Murder by the Person who ordered the Military to fire," which Verdict the Coroner refused to receive; and the Jurors were, after some time, induced to return a second Verdict, as above.]

Thomas Morgan.—Verdict, Wilful Murder by Person or Persons unknown.

Humphrey Lewis, of Castle-Carey.—Verdict, Wilful Murder by Person or Persons unknown.

John Jones, Accomptant.—Verdict, Wilful Murder by Person or Persons unknown.

Anthony Gill, Shoemaker, Parish of St. James, aged 34.—Verdict, Wilful Murder by Person or Persons unknown.

James Bennet, aged 22, Parish of St. Mary Redcliff.—Verdict, Accidental Death.

Isaac Davis, aged 18, Parish of St. Thomas.—Verdict, Wilful Murder by Person or Persons unknown.

Elizabeth Kegan, aged 55, Parish of St. Stephen.—Verdict, Wilful Murder by Person or Persons unknown.

A LIST OF THE WOUNDED.

OF REDCLIFF PARISH.

Harriet Davis, aged 13, gun-shot wound in the Thigh.
Sarah Silcox, aged 55, wound in the Thigh.
Eliz. Hichens, aged 16, wound in the Foot.
Dan. Bishop, aged 20, wound in the Arm.
Jane Thomas, aged 18, wound in the Foot.
Stephen Cox, aged 19, wound in the Thigh.

OF TEMPLE PARISH.

Joseph White, aged 44, gun-shot wound in the Side.
Henry Knotley, aged 24, wound in the Leg and Arm.
Thomas Knotley, aged 22, wound in the Thighs.
Caleb Love, aged 51, amputated Arm.
Richard Ponsford, aged 32, wound in the Thigh.
Thomas Stephens, aged 18, wound in the Thigh.
Thomas Smith, aged 23, wound in the Leg.
Michael Nelson, aged 22, wound in the Head.
John Alexander, aged 42, wound through the Leg.
William Davis, aged 22, wound in the Ancle.
Robert Hughes, aged 18, wound in the Shoulder.

OF ST. THOMAS PARISH.

William Thomson, aged 29, gun-shot wound in the Arm.
Richard Cole, aged 17, wound in the Thigh.
Mary Knight, aged 46, wound in the Foot.

OF THE PARISH OF ST. PHILIP AND JACOB.

Esther Nash, aged 19, gun-shot wound in the Leg.
John Hookins, aged 19, wound in the Thigh.
James Jarrett, aged 22, wound in the Shoulder.
Benjamin Parish, aged 45, wound in the Hand.
Samuel Hopkins, aged 23, wound in the Face.

OF THE PARISH OF ST. JAMES.

Thomas Powell, aged 18, gun-shot wound in the Head.
William Anstice, aged 21, wound in the Hand.
Thomas Hedgland, aged 34, wound in the Hand.
Malachi Norris, aged 43, contused Eye.
Thomas Rossiter, aged 45, grazed Forehead.

OF THE PARISH OF ST. STEPHEN.

—— *Davis,* aged 50, gun-shot wound in the Knee.
Thomas Coles, aged 38, wound in the Leg.

OF THE PARISH OF ST. NICHOLAS.

William Puddicomb, aged 32, gun-shot wounds in the Wrist and Hip.
Margaret Morgan, aged 49, wound in the Heel.
William Burleigh, aged 14, wound in the Foot.
William Wrestill, aged 28, Parish of St. Maryport, gun-shot wound in the Legs.
William Horwood, aged 20, Parish of St. George, gun-shot wounds in the Groin and Hand.
Charles Coole, aged 25, Parish of Bitton, gun-shot wound in the Abdomen.
William Groves, aged 20, Parish of St. Paul, gun-shot wound in the Wrist.
John Lloyd, aged 17, gun-shot wound in the Face.
Daniel Pierce, aged about 15, gun-shot wounds in the Foot and Heel.
Thomas Baynham, aged about 26, sabre wound in the Hand.
Thomas Foxall, aged about 17, *Bridgnorth,* bayonet wound in the Hand.
Thomas Parke, aged about 27, gun-shot wound through the Shoulder.
William Alwick, aged about 27, gun-shot wound through the Thigh.
Henry Edminston, aged about 35, gun-shot wound through the Arm.
James Edwards, aged about 32, gun-shot wound in the Leg.
Robert Hewett, aged about 40, gun-shot wound in the Face.
Thomas Rogers, aged about 42, gun-shot wound in the Loin.
James Harris, aged about 23, gun-shot wound in the Knee.
John Kingdom, aged about 22, Parish of Bedminster, gun-shot wounds in the Hand and Thigh.
—— *Jenkins,* aged about 29, Parish of St. Peter, gun-shot wound in the Shoulder.

N. B. Several of the Wounded have since Died.

[Price TWO-PENCE.]

Handbill Bill, 1793. Slaughter on Bristol Bridge: a bloody day in Bristol's history. Five weeks after the massacre the total number of fatal casualties had risen to 14. (Bristol Reference Library)

74

increasingly violent. At the approach of dusk it was thought wise to allow free passage until the following day. On Monday, however, the commissioners resumed their attempts to collect the toll. But being constantly harassed and abused they had little success and many people fought their way across the bridge without paying. Several people were also arrested and taken to the Bridewell, an act which only served to increase the anger of the crowd. Eventually the Riot Act was read out three times but was met merely by hoots of derision. The magistrates, who so far had restrained themselves from recalling the military, at last felt compelled to summon further support and at midday warned that: 'Those who will not be advised must take the consequence, that if they receive any injury it must lay upon their own heads.'

On their arrival, the Herefordshire Regiment, under strict orders to show restraint, were pelted with stones and oyster shells. Again, as dusk approached the magistrates decided to close the bridge and shut up the toll house so as to avoid further confrontation. But as soon as the soldiers withdrew, the crowd went on the rampage; the toll house was broken into and its furniture was thrown onto a bonfire that was soon blazing on the bridge. One anonymous pamphlet writer later observed that the fire served to fuel the anger of the crowd:

'Every man of observation knows that there is such a natural connection between a bonfire and mobbing, to the common people of England, that it is, in general necessary only to form one in order to create the other.' [24]

The soldiers were hastily brought back to the bridge and ordered to fire on the crowd to disperse it. With no further warning the soldiers fired along St Thomas Street. Despite their volleys southward the soldiers continued to be attacked from the north in the direction of the High Street. The soldiers about turned and fired along the High Street. On that night eleven people were killed and another forty-five were injured. Over the weeks that followed another three of the injured were to die – bringing the total number of fatal casualties to 14. [25]

Strangely, there was a rumour circulating that the soldiers could not legally fire at the mob; if they did it was thought that they must use only powder and not shot. The fatal consequence was that few of the crowd dispersed when the militia fired southward. This point of view was held by Bristol historian John Evans, who was an eye witness:

'The writer was at this instant between seven and eight in professional attendance at the theatre but so strongly was he possessed of the belief that only powder had been discharged, of which some of the flying mob, whom he first met near the Back Hall, repeatedly assured him that he passed one man lying prostrate, as if fallen in flight through inebriety, at the foot of St Nicholas church steps…and with unabated security, another man lying near the place of the watchbox in the church yard railing, from whom a stream issued down the pavement.' [26]

It would seem that either Evans was exceptionally shortsighted – which he was not – or he had the utmost faith in the placidity of the soldiers, for these were not drunken bodies that he was stepping over, but corpses. Oblivious that he was walking through a battlefield Evans calmly continued on his way home even though:

'A bonfire blazed on the bridge and the firing of musketry and the roll of drums had not ceased on the side of St Thomas Street.' [27]

The slaughter on Bristol Bridge is a bloody and shameful day in Bristol's history. Admittedly the soldiers had suffered prolonged harassment for several days but even this was little excuse for their indiscriminate firing. Prior to the massacre the Riot Act had not been read for several hours during which time a number of spectators had gathered to watch the mob's antics. Many innocent bystanders were injured during the discharge; three women from the parishes of Redcliffe and St Thomas were hurt whilst a visitor from Castle Cary who was merely passing through the city at the time was killed.

The inflammatory behaviour of the magistrates and the bridge commissioners caused a national outcry. In Bristol, the coroner's courts expressed their extreme disapproval by passing a verdict of *'wilful murder by persons unknown'* on ten of the victims. Yet the situation was not straightforward. In the absence of an established police force, when large scale violence threatened there was no alternative but to call out the military. Such a decision was never easy to take, for subsequent events might prove that the problem did not justify military intervention. Also, the justices were notoriously keen to punish any soldier accused of using undue force against a civilian. Thus soldiers ordered to fire upon a crowd might well be accused of murder if they obeyed, or if they disobeyed, be shot themselves for mutiny.

And of course, members of the crowd were not blameless. A demonstration always offers a chance for the more disruptive elements of society to take revenge against authority and doubtless this demonstration was no exception. Besides, across Europe the French Revolution of 1789 had roused a real feeling that the toppling of old inequalities was possible. In England, even though the common individual was powerless, the common mass was capable of a good deal of noise and sometimes violence. This violence, or threat of it, was sometimes the only way that the voice of the working person could be heard.

Despite claims by the Corporation that it was 'neither wise nor salutary' and 'was a dangerous concession to the populace'[28] the dispute over the tolls was finally settled when a number of citizens joined together to pay off the remaining debts. The Corporation, mindful of the guillotine that had recently been set up in the Place de la Revolution, Paris, warily dismissed the idea of any further enquiry into the massacre by denouncing the promoters of such an investigation as 'revolutionaries.' The Minute Book of the Proceedings of the Common Council is suspiciously lacking in any direct reference to the

Samuel Taylor Coleridge. The young poet was married in St. Mary Redcliffe in 1795.
He later lived in "pent up rooms" in Redcliffe Hill.
(National Portrait Gallery)

trouble. Indeed, while Bristol was on the verge of burning it appears the councillors were calmly discussing the price of turbot.[29]

COLERIDGE'S EARLY DAYS IN BRISTOL

In the 1770s Chatterton had found the cold wind of indifference to his talent too harsh and moved to London to seek fame and fortune. Times were changing, however. To the editors of Defoe's 1778 guide, the city had altered almost beyond recognition. 'Its gentry, merchants and capital traders are polite and superb in their town and country houses, equipages, servants and amusements as any in the Kingdom.' They added that there was now an element of culture to be found in the city: 'Literature and genteel education are much cultivated in Bristol; and it abounds with agreeable women whose modes of dress are universally approved.' Only one thing rankled though, for even behind all this finery the Bristol accent could not be disguised. Although Defoe's guide admitted that 'People of rank and education here, as everywhere else, pronounce with propriety' it had to be said that other members of the trading classes spoke in a 'broad dialect much worse than the common people in the metropolis.'[30]

If Chatterton had been born twenty years later he would have found that the presence in Bristol of the formidable Hannah More (a best selling writer in her time, but now considered unreadable) acted as a magnet to other literati. One such person was the young poet Samuel Taylor Coleridge.

Coleridge had been influenced to move to Bristol by the future Poet Laureate Robert Southey. Together they were advocates of the unfortunately named Pantisocratic scheme which involved a communal search for Utopia – it was all part of the idealism that was sweeping Europe after the French Revolution. Coleridge and his fellows proposed a plan where a dozen or so 'kindred spirits,' along with their wives, would move to a settlement on the banks of the Susquehanna (they liked the sound of the name), in North America and establish a commune.

There they thought the good life would come easily. A mere three or four hours work a day would make the group self sufficient. The rest of the time would be spent in literary and artistic pursuits.

Whilst waiting for converts to the scheme, Coleridge busied himself by writing radical lectures which, for a small fee, he would present at the Pelican Inn in Thomas Street and various other inns in the city. Although his talk of revolution was rarely passively received he was well able to defend himself with acid wit against hecklers. On one occasion a hostile audience expressed their disapproval by hissing. Coleridge quickly retorted:

'I am not at all surprised that when the red hot prejudices are plunged into cold water they should go off with a hiss.'

His audiences were also amused by his dragged-through-a-hedge-backwards appearance. A local journal wrote:

'His speech is a perfect monotonism, his person is slovenly... Mr Coleridge would do well to appear in cleaner stockings and if his hair were combed out every time he appeared in public it would not deprecate him in the esteem of his friends.' [31]

The Pantisocratists were all to be partnered in their Utopian world and to this end they descended upon the daughters of the widowed Mrs Fricker. Poor Mrs Fricker found that her daughters were every Pantisocratist's dream and they were duly courted.

Robert Lovell, a member of the group had already married one of the Frickers. Robert Southey became engaged to another, Burnet was engaged to a third (she eventually had second thoughts about it realising that he only wanted 'a wife in a hurry') and on September 4th, 1795 Coleridge and Sara Fricker were married in St Mary Redcliffe. After the wedding the young couple went on a protracted honeymoon to the seaside village of Clevedon.

After two months in sleepy Clevedon it comes as no surprise that Coleridge was straining to return to Bristol. He felt that he could no longer remain on his honeymoon whilst 'his unnumbered brethren toiled and bled.'

Coleridge's marriage to Sara could not be described as happy. They married in a blur of idealism; but with time the haze cleared, yet to Coleridge's dismay the marriage bonds remained. Coleridge was not an easy person to live with – even in these early days he was addicted to laudanum, the alcoholic tincture of opium, and consequently subject to unpredictable extremes of mood.[32] Sara was also the victim of malicious gossip amongst Coleridge's literary colleagues. As the poet Shelley was to observe of the Fricker sisters: 'Mrs Southey is stupid; Mrs Coleridge worse.'

They moved back to Bristol into pent-up rooms with Mrs Fricker in Redcliffe Hill and from there Coleridge dabbled in journalism, publishing a political rag called the *Watchman*. The magazine, whose motto was 'All might know the truth and the truth might make them free' was intended to stimulate political discussion; in fact the immature and contradictory ramblings served more to muddle than to educate. This confusion was aggravated by the decision to publish every eighth day. Although this avoided stamp tax, the magazine confounded its readers by appearing on different days of the week. After ten issues the paper folded and Coleridge elegized – 'O Watchman thou hast watched in vain.'

Undaunted by the lack of converts for the commune and the failure of the magazine, Coleridge turned his attention to something that was to be of more lasting value – the production of his first book of poems. Prior to his arrival in Bristol, Coleridge had offered

*Inspired by his wife's dream the plumber Mr Watts built the world's first shot
tower on Redcliffe Hill in 1782. Demolished 1967.
(City of Bristol Museum and Art Gallery)*

works to various publishers in London. The best advance to be had was six guineas. Impoverished though he was, the poet was not willing to accept such a miserable fee.

In Bristol, however, the bookseller Joseph Cottle was able to promise a healthy advance of £30. Subsequently there were times when Cottle regretted his benevolence, for Coleridge's procrastination could try even the most patient. Cottle was repeatedly obliged to remind the poet of his commitment. In return Coleridge would send back notes to his publisher explaining his tardiness. His messages ranged from the optimistic: 'I have been composing in the fields this morning' to dramatic excuses: 'A devil, a very devil, has got possession of my left temple, eye, cheek, jaw and shoulder…I write in agony.' [33]

The Coleridges left Redcliffe Hill in March 1796 and moved to Oxford Street in Kingsdown.

After much delay the book was published in April 1797. It proved that Coleridge was not merely a hot headed hedonist but also a serious poet and was to pave the way for the works of genius that were to follow.

MRS WATTS' DREAM

Apart from Chatterton and Coleridge, Redcliffe Hill also boasts the residence of another visionary, the plumber's wife, Mrs Watts.

In 1782, Mr Watts, a plumber of Redcliffe Hill, patented a new and startlingly simple process for the manufacture of lead shot. The lead that had been mined in the Mendips since Roman times had given rise to a small lead smelting industry in Bristol. Prior to Mr Watts' new process, lead shot had been laboriously cast in moulds. Like all great inventions the idea behind the new technique was simple. Basically it involved pouring molten lead through a sieve and into a vat of water below. The blobs of lead cooled by the water, formed perfectly spherical balls. Manufactured by this process Mr Watts' lead shot was of good quality and cheap to produce.

There are various tales as to who stumbled across this process, for both Mr Watts and his wife have been accredited with the original inspiration. Mr Watts was allegedly inspired by a dream in which molten lead was pouring from the roof of a burning St Mary Redcliffe. As the lead hit the wet ground it formed into lead shot. Mrs Watts, however, is also reputed to be the visionary. The story is told that in her dream she saw lead pouring from the top landing of her staircase into a container of water below. When she looked into the water she was surprised to find it contained lead shot. She awoke from her sleep and immediately roused her husband and excitedly told him about her dream. Mr Watts, who was unenthusiastic about his wife's wild rantings in the middle of the night, muttered something about 'the folly of dreams' and went straight back to sleep. Mrs Watts also fell asleep but her dreaming continued. Again she woke her husband who was so infuriated by this second interruption to his well earned sleep that he could not help expressing himself in 'somewhat strong saxon.' The next morning in the calm of the day, Mr Watts pondered his wife's dream and thought that there might well be something in it.[34]

Whoever had the dream doesn't matter – what is important is that the process worked. With experiment it was found that the size of lead shot produced depended on the length of the drop. The larger the shot, the longer the drop required. Mr Watts was so sure of the value of the invention he converted his house for production. First, he knocked out the floors and ceilings of his living accommodation and then above this, to gain a 60 ft drop, he built a tower. To make even larger shot, he doubled the drop by digging down below his house into Redcliffe Caves.

Soon Mr Watts' business was doing so well that he was able to make further plans for expansion. A newspaper announced that the inventor was about to enlarge his premises with the erection of a new 'gothic tower.' This structure, alongside the other tower, was to be designed in such an elegant manner that the view of the building was expected to remind the spectator of Westminster Abbey! The expectations were somewhat overstated for the original tower was exceedingly plain, if not ugly, its only embellishment being a castellated top.

But the tower was never built; Mr Watts turned his attention to the fad of speculative building that was raging in the city and Clifton at the time. Mr Watts unwisely invested £10,000 in the development of Windsor Terrace in Clifton. With its steeply sloping terrain it was a precarious building site and most of Mr Watts' money was spent on merely securing the foundations. By 1792 his funds were exhausted and he was forced to offer the building for sale in an unfinished state.

In 1794, the bankrupt Mr Watts, having sold his lead shot business to Philip George (the founder of George's Brewery) disappeared into obscurity. Nevertheless Mr Watts' invention lives on; the original shot tower continued in use till 1967. Even today, Sheldon Bush's modern shot tower (now itself sadly obsolete) which dominates the skyline of central Bristol, is a reminder of a two hundred year old vision.

Notes

1. W.S. Lewis (ed.) *Horace Walpole's Correspondence* (1941), Vol X, p.232
2. J.H. Bettey, *Bristol Observed* (Redcliffe Press, 1986) p.67
3. S. Hutton, *Bristol and its Famous Associations* (1907) p.48
4. P. McGrath, *'Bristol since 1497'* in *Bristol and its Adjoining Counties* (ed. MacInnes and Whittard, 1955) p.214
5. I.V. Hall, *Temple Street Sugar House under the first Partnership of Richard Lane and John Hine, 1662 1678* (B.G.A. 76.1957) p.1286
6. Cyril Weedon, *'The Bristol Bottlemakers'* Chemistry and Industry (June 3rd, 1978) p.378
7. ibid. p.379
8. P.T. Marcy, *'18th Century Views of Bristol and Bristolians' Bristol in the 18th Century* (ed. P. McGrath, Newton Abbot, 1972) p.16
9. H.E. Mathews, *The Company of Soapmakers* (Bristol Record Society) p.196

10. P. Roger, *Defoe, John Oldmixon and the Bristol Riots of 1714* (B.G.A.S., 1973) p.145146
11. J. Evans, *A Chronological Outline of the History of Bristol* (1824) p.256-257
12. Sarah Farley's Journal July 29th, 1749
13. *Bristol Journal*, August 12th, 1749
14. J. Latimer, *Annals of 18th Century Bristol* (1893) p.269
15. ibid, p.367
16. R.C. Tombs, *The Bristol Post* (1899) p.20
17. S. Hutton, op cit, p.48
18. Felix Farley's *Bristol Journal*, February 6th, 1747
19. P.T. Marcy, *Bristol's Roads and Communications on the Eve of the Industrial Revolution* (B.G.A.S.,1968) Vol.87, p.152
20. J. Latimer, op cit, p.175
21. J.A. Spring and D.H. Buss, *Nature* (December 15th, 1977) Vol. 270
22. Boswell's *Life of Johnson* (Globe Edition) p.370
23. B. Cottle, *'Thomas Chatterton',* in P. McGrath, Bristol in the 18th Century (1972) p.104
24. Anon., *An Impartial History of the Late Riots in Bristol*, p.9
25. M. Manson, *'Riot!' The Bristol Bridge Massacre of 1793* (Past and Present Press, 1997) p.75
26. J. Evans, op cit, p.300
27. ibid, p.300
28. Anon., *An Impartial History of the Late Riots in Bristol*, p.14
29. *Minutes of the Proceedings of the Common Council*, Saturday 29 September 1793. Bristol Reference Library B13065
30. P.T. Marcy, *'Views of Bristol and Bristolians,'* Bristol in the 18th Century, p.36
31. M. Carpenter, *The Indifferent Horseman*, p.63
32. M. Lefevre, *The Bondage of Love* (London, 1986) p.54
33. J. Cottle, *Reminiscences of Coleridge and Southey* (London, 1848) p.37
34. *Work in Bristol*, Bristol (1883) p.187

Other Sources

B. Cottle, *'Thomas Chatterton,'* in *Bristol in the 18th Century* (ed. McGrath)
John Dix, *Life of Chatterton* (London, 1837)
W. Ison, *The Georgian Buildings of Bristol* (London)
P.T. Marcy, *Bristol's Roads and Communications on the Eve of the Industrial Revolution* (B.G.A.S., 1968) Vol 86, p.149172
W.J. Pountney, *Old Bristol Potteries* (Bristol, 1920)
C. Witt, C. Weeden, A. Palmer Schwind, *Bristol Glass* (Redcliffe Press, 1984)
C. Witt, *'Good Cream Color Ware',* in The Connoisseur (September, 1979)

FIVE

THE FLOATING HARBOUR

The findings of the first official census of England in 1801 were a disappointment to Bristolians. It had always been believed that the city, with its self-estimated population of over 100,000, was second only to London in the number of its inhabitants. In fact, the national census judged Bristol's population – at a mere 65,645 – to be much lower. The census only proved what many well-travelled people had already guessed: that Bristol had slipped well behind its rival Liverpool as holder of the cherished position of second city in the nation. Despite the war with America, Liverpool had grown so rapidly after 1775 that Bristol was not able to compete. Liverpool's dynamic expansion was largely due to the success of the cotton trade in Lancashire that produced an increase in both imports and exports.

Meanwhile at the beginning of the nineteenth century the prospects for Bristol did not look good: its trade hinterland was shrinking; its merchants seemed drained of the dynamism that so characterised Bristol's Golden Age and its docks were antiquated.

A change in the national economy was affecting Bristol's local trading position. With the development of the canals, several industries that had traditionally depended on Bristol were able to use services nearer at hand. Bristol was now no longer the 'Welsh metropolis' for the Welsh were developing their own ports.

But in many ways Bristol's merchants had only themselves to blame. It was largely their own attitudes to trade that contributed to this stagnation. They were conservative and content to rest on the laurels of their past achievements. Having enjoyed a healthy and prosperous trade for so long Bristol's merchants no longer looked to expand. Bristol was moving at a slower pace than the hustling, bustling cities of the north that had become the workshop of the world.

Surprisingly, American Independence (1776) and the outlawing of the slave trade (1807) had less of an adverse effect on Bristol's trade than might have been expected. Bristol's involvement with the American War of Independence was only half hearted. In reality Bristolians were not interested in the matter of sovereignty – they wanted trade. With regards to slavery, Bristol's share in the trade had long been dwarfed by Liverpool's – indeed some Bristolians and their parliamentary representative, Edmund Burke, played an active role in the anti-slavery campaign. Although the transportation of Africans was made illegal, Bristolians still benefited from the products of their enforced labour – as late

*Entrance to Bathurst Basin. Floating Harbour completed 1809: smaller vessels were able
to sail up The Cut and enter through a lock into the Bathurst Basin.
(City of Bristol Museum and Art Gallery)*

as 1833 one prominent Bristol merchant was to say that without the West Indian trade in slaves and sugar Bristol would have been a mere fishing port.

Even so, the decline of Bristol's trading position was further hastened by the condition of the city's inadequate and old-fashioned dock facilities. Only with great difficulty could they handle the large ocean-going ships that plied the Atlantic. For a long time efforts had been made to improve the shipping accommodation offered by the port – plans had first been drawn up in 1765 – but it was not until the full implications of the census had sunk in that the matter was considered seriously.

On a local level, there was, at first, persistent opposition to any radical changes in the harbour. At a parish meeting held in Redcliffe in May 1803 the view that a new floating harbour 'would ultimately destroy the present Accommodation of the Port, and would be the ruin of our commerce and trade' was typical of the conservative argument. More to the point perhaps, was the indignation expressed when it was realised that a rise in house rates would accompany any such scheme. The Redcliffe meeting concluded that the advantages of a floating harbour 'must be very remote.'

Despite the opposition of local parishioners, the new harbour development went ahead. Designed by William Jessop, one of the main objectives was to remove the inconvenience caused by the ebb and flow of the tide. Jessop's plan was to dig a new channel for the Avon – The Cut – while converting, with the aid of locks and dams, the original course of the river into a two and a half mile floating harbour. The main entrance into the float was to be through the Cumberland Basin lock gates. Smaller vessels would be able to sail up The Cut and enter through a side entrance into the triangular Bathurst Basin (named after the MP for Bristol, 1796-1807) which covered the former site of the Treen Mills and Malago Brook.

Jessop's design was not original – in fact it suspiciously echoed a similar proposal put forward in 1791 by the vicar of Temple Church, the Reverend Mitton. The Dock Company was reluctant to admit this, and only very grudgingly did they acknowledge that their plan owed anything to Mitton's original inspiration. As a sop they did, however, award the Reverend with 'a piece of plate not exceeding the value of one hundred guineas.'[1]

On a scale that matched the medieval dock improvements, the building of the Floating Harbour was an undertaking that demanded a large labour force. Six hundred and four navvies started work in 1804 but by the end of the project their numbers had swollen to over a thousand. (Regardless of a long standing tradition that The Cut was dug by French prisoners, there are in fact no records to verify this.) Progress was slow and it soon became clear that the cost and length of the task had been seriously underestimated. In the end the works took over a year longer, and cost twice as much, as originally planned.

At last, precisely five years after its inauguration, the Docks Company was proud, and somewhat relieved, to announce that:

'after struggling through numberless unforeseen difficulties, both local and accidental . . . after having perhaps undertaken to perform in a given time more than it appears

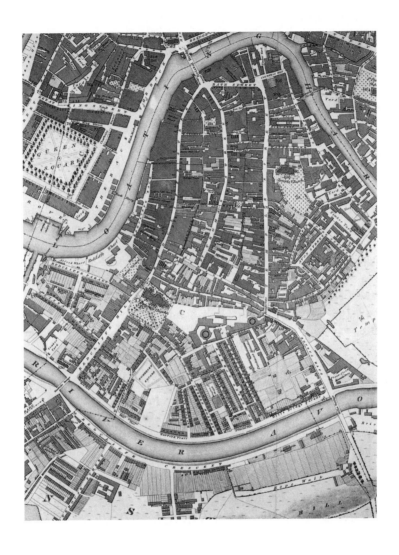

*Part of Ashmead's Map of Bristol in 1823. Gardens and yards have been built over
– landlords utilised every inch, cramming dwellings into any little space available.
(City of Bristol Museum and Art Gallery)*

possible in the capacity of human art to execute, the directors of this concern have fulfilled their engagement.' [2]

The construction of the Floating Harbour had finally been completed.

To celebrate the event the directors of the Dock Company treated the labourers to a dinner.

'In the good old style of English hospitality,' *Felix Farley's Bristol Journal* cheerfully reported, 'two whole oxen, 6 cwt of plum pudding, 1,000 gallons of stingo and other things in proportion had been provided.'

But as the stingo was consumed, emotions rose. The *Journal* carried on to report that 'the people indulged themselves of all the graceful eccentricities of liberty.' However, 'upon the arrival of a cart with a fresh supply of ale, some honest Hibernians proceeded rather unceremoniously to disburthen the vehicle of its contents.' The sight of the sack of the beer wagon was just too much for the patience of the 'John Bulls' and soon a full-scale drunken brawl broke out. The dinner, now turned riot, was only 'terminated by the interference of the police and the press gang; but not without taking one party of combatants to Bridewell' [3].

Though the Floating Harbour was completed in 1809 little economic benefit was derived from it for many years. The Dock Company insisted on a good return for its investment by the imposition of unrealistically high rates. A great deal of business must have been lost for the levies were extortionate: they exceeded those paid at Liverpool by 60 per cent and London by 115 per cent.

The Floating Harbour was a grand undertaking and even today it is an epic monument to the spirit of nineteenth century engineering. It is still virtually intact and now represents the very heart and character of the city of Bristol. But even so, this show of confidence was not enough to halt the downward turn in the city's trade – in reality the building of the Floating Harbour turned out to be the port's swansong.

'AN EXTENSIVE AND COMMODIOUS BUILDING'

'This is an extensive and commodious building,' wrote the editor of the 1825 *Mathew's Bristol, Clifton and Hotwell Guide*, 'which for health convenience and excellent arrangement is not to be equalled in England, commanding extensive views of the surrounding countryside…The boundary wall (20 feet high) is built in hewn variegated marble which has a beautiful appearance.' What was this handsome construction? An hotel in Clifton? Or perhaps a new commercial citadel? In fact, the writer of the guide was describing Bristol's latest contribution to progressive thinking – The New Gaol.

Prior to 1820 Bristol's two prisons – Bridewell and Newgate – were housed in buildings most unsuited to their use. Of the whitewashed Newgate, John Howard, the outspoken eighteenth century prison reformer wrote 'it is white without and foul within.' It was largely due to the pressures exerted by such selfless agitators as Howard that attention focused towards the end of the century on the national scandal of the country's prisons. But it was a slow process. Howard visited Bristol in 1774, and in spite of his public protests very few improvements were made. The insalubrity of the Bridewell is emphasised by the fact that a cat had to be kept in the cells at night to stop rats and mice from gnawing the prisoners' feet.

However, in 1816, after a series of enquiries and reports the Corporation at last proposed that a new gaol should be built at a cost of £60,000. A piece of land away from the more crowded areas (just outside the Redcliffe Parish Boundary) and sandwiched between The Cut and the Floating Harbour was chosen for the site – the vicinity today is still known colloquially as Spike Island. The building of the gaol was finished in August 1820 when the first prisoners were transported by wagon from Newgate, the Bridewell continuing in use.

Unquestionably the New Gaol was a great advance on the buildings that it superseded and was held up as a model to be emulated across the country. It was designed to hold 197 prisoners, all to be kept in single cells measuring six feet by nine feet. Facilities were such (and this was unusual) that the prisoners were expected to be able to wash their hands and faces and comb their hair daily and even bath once a month.

The water for their ablutions was to come from an inexhaustible well one hundred feet deep, the water being raised by a treadmill. The treadmill, or cockchaffer as it was euphemistically called, was a familiar feature of nineteenth century penal institutions. The New Gaol was equipped with treadmills for twenty persons – besides drawing water the treadmills were also used for grinding corn.

Both sexes were catered for in the prison – but were to be strictly segregated. The female prisoners were supervised by a matron and no male warders were allowed to visit the female prisoners unless accompanied by the matron or another female officer.

The granite gatehouse with its mock portcullis was equipped with a flat roof and a trap door specifically designed for executions. Executions were, of course, public affairs – and good crowd pullers at that. This could cause a problem as space for spectators was limited by the New Cut which was just across the road from the gatehouse. At the first public execution, in 1821, of a young lad sentenced for killing his girlfriend there was such a crush that notices had to be put up warning people to beware of being pushed into the unfenced Avon.[5]

As exemplary as the prison was, by 1840 conditions had, for a variety of reasons, declined. A report by the visiting magistrates published in 1841 is reminiscent of the bad old days; much of the damage from the 1831 Riots had never been rectified, conditions were overcrowded and unpleasant, and discipline was lax.

For a start, the magistrates found the so-called inexhaustible supply of water to be undrinkable, while the much vaunted availability of baths was non existent. Many of the

The New Gaol (opened 1820) "an extensive and commodious building which for convenience and excellent arrangement is not to be equalled in England" was held up as a model to be emulated across the country.
(City of Bristol Museum and Art Gallery)

prisoners were poorly clothed against the winter cold and some even had no shoes or other footwear. Also, due to the smallness of the windows, the air-supply in the prison was static, the atmosphere consequently becoming stale and fetid. On the other hand many of the cells had unglazed iron windows with wooden shutters; in the winter the prisoners were compelled either to be shut in darkness or suffer the cold.

Additionally the magistrates noted that the supervision of the prison at night-time was difficult as, apart from times of a clear sky and a bright moon, the buildings were swathed in darkness. The installation of gas lamps was therefore recommended.

The magistrates had already ordered food allowances to be increased: 'five ounces of dressed meat to be given twice a week, soup twice a week, and larger portions of bread when meat was not allowed.' Lest the magistrates were thought of as soft or extravagant, they felt compelled to point out that they were only meeting the requirements laid down by the Secretary of State, adding that due to this new dietary regime 'far less sickness is to be found in the prison.' [6]

And finally, with regards to security, the Justices found the prison to be grossly understaffed. There was one clerk and just six warders, or turnkeys as they were called, for both day and night duty, and only one female officer to act as matron. Not surprisingly the segregation of the sexes had proved impossible. It was even claimed that two female prisoners had become pregnant by one of the warders – who had subsequently absconded. Security being of the utmost importance, even by the time the Justice's report had been published, the number of staff had been increased to twentythree.

With more staff, the Justices were able to operate their 'new system' of discipline within the gaol. It had long been recognised that prison was not so much a place of correction but more a college of crime. 'To commit a fellow creature to jail in its present state,' wrote the magistrates in 1837, 'is to consign him to almost irretrievable infamy and ruin.' The 'new system,' however consisted of minimising the contact of fellow prisoners so that they lived in virtual solitary confinement. According to an enthusiastic report of 1841 the new arrangements were so successful that 'we know of one hundred and one prisoners tried and convicted since this new system was enforced, who now honestly earn their bread by the sweat of their brow, and appear to be thoroughly reformed characters.' Indeed, no less an authority than the Deputy Lieutenant of the County of Cork backed up this claim by writing that 'having devoted many years to the improvement of my own county gaol, and for this purpose (having) closely examined many gaols in England and on the continent, I feel confident in stating that I have seen none equal to the Bristol gaol.'

Despite this glowing report, over the following years conditions yet again deteriorated. In 1872 the Home Office remonstrated with the Corporation that the prison was unfit for its purpose. The gaol was in such a state of decay that nothing could be done except to start building yet again. Accordingly the Corporation bought some land north of the city at Horfield Gardens but wisely procrastinated from doing anything further. Bristol was

The gatehouse with its flat roof and 'drop' for public executions is all that remains of the prison today.
(Photo M. Manson)

spared the expense of building another prison when, in 1878, the Home Office took over responsibility for penal institutions across the country.

All that remains of the New Gaol today – it was last used in 1883 and sold to the Great Western Railway in 1895 – is the flat roofed grey gatehouse beside the Cumberland Road, and a few yards of wall that is incorporated into the buildings of a coal merchant.

ANARCHY AND ANGER

On the morning of Saturday, October 29th, 1831 Bristol's Recorder, Sir Charles Wetherall, arrived to open the Quarter Sessions. Wetherall's presence in the city signaled the beginning of the Bristol Riots, a short period of rebellion that was to both shatter the city and stun the nation. In the days that followed, Bristol experienced a sustained riot that has since remained unequalled in England's history; for the next three days anarchy and anger were to rule the city.

What sparked off this explosion of lawlessness? The upset caused by Wetherall's arrival in Bristol must be viewed against a wider backdrop of both local and national discontent. The mob's targets over the next few days were to give an indication of where some of the local problems lay. As Lord Byron had said to the House of Lords: 'You may call the people a mob; but do not forget that the mob often speaks the sentiments of the people.' Thus attacks upon the Mansion House, the prisons and the Bishop's Palace were all expressions of long standing grievances. Unemployment was certainly one reason for discontent. Some believed that ever since the construction of the Floating Harbour wages had dropped and jobs had become scarce. During the riots the Luddite cry was frequently heard to 'cut down the lock gates.'

The greatest amount of hatred was, however, reserved for the Corporation. The Corporation had become so aloof and remote from the working classes that its workings were generally regarded with suspicion. Where was the rate money going? Whose interests were really being looked after? To many, the Corporation was seen merely as an openly wasteful clan, a self electing secretive clique, that indulged itself at the cost of the rate payers, in numerous official dinners, ceremonies and other extravagances. In the slowly deteriorating parishes of Redcliffe, Temple and St Thomas it was generally thought that the rates could be put to better use than these shows of pomp and civic pride.

There were also national problems. 1831 was the year of the controversial debate on Parliamentary Reform. Due to the rapid growth of population in some parts of the country large areas had found themselves without representation in Westminster. The House of Lords' eventual rejection of an electoral reform that would rectify, to a certain extent, this inequality had caused a national uproar. One person who had openly been opposed to reform was Wetherall.

Even at the best of times Wetherall was an unpopular man. Indeed, the London newspaper the *Morning Chronicle* had gone so far as to call him 'the most detested man in the Kingdom' [8]. To make matters worse, because he held the office of Recorder in Bristol, Wetherall had recently taken it upon himself to speak in Parliament on behalf of the city. According to a reformist writer he asserted himself in a most unusual manner. It was reported during the Reform debate that:

> *'The conduct of Sir Charles Wetherall, at all times eccentric, was during the discussion of the Reform Bill in the House of Commons the most extraordinary that has ever been witnessed, even in that place.'*

Wetherall was jumping the mark here, for far from being Bristol's elected member he merely represented a small rural parish in Yorkshire, a rotten borough, that was due to disappear if the Reform Bill was passed.

So the riots were not entirely unexpected. Indeed, during the previous twelve months there had been numerous large and sometimes boisterous Sunday political meetings in Queen Square. A few days prior to the riots the Council, sensing that trouble was brewing, had taken steps to recruit special constables. Unfortunately their appeal for help from the more respectable members of society fell upon deaf ears (in itself a measure of the council's unpopularity) and eventually one hundred and seventeen less suitable 'bludgeon men' were recruited. It was Wetherall's presence in Bristol that was to act as a final catalyst to emotions that were already running high.

As Wetherall's coach pressed on down Temple Street it was almost hemmed in by a mud slinging, jeering crowd. Even though the Corn Street courts were heavily guarded it was felt that the opening of the assize would be unwise against such a volatile background.

The Judge therefore hastily made his way to an official luncheon with the Mayor in the Mansion House in Queen Square.

As a large and jostling crowd quickly gathered outside the Mansion House it was obvious that if the situation were to be contained a calming influence was required. Unfortunately, the special constables tended to inflame matters rather than soothe them. The last thing that was needed was a heavy-handed bunch of ill-disciplined special constables throwing their weight around. Consequently there were sporadic outbreaks of fighting as a group of 'specials' unwisely made some arrests.

The shouts of the crowd in Queen Square were soon punctuated by the sound of shattering glass as the windows of the Mansion House were broken and the iron railings torn down. The Mayor, Charles Pinney, a reformist, and therefore not unpopular with the crowd, attempted to address the throng. But they were in no mood to listen and eventually the Riot Act was read with no effect – the increasingly restless crowd merely responded with jeers and catcalls. Then, after the special constables had been brutally disarmed, a number of the mob broke into the ground floor of the Mansion House and looted furniture, food and drink. One of the ringleaders, Christopher Davis of The Counterslip, Temple Parish tucked into the banquet that had been prepared for the Mayor and Recorder saying 'what a shame it is that there should be so much waste when so many poor wretches are starving.' Wetherall, meanwhile, realising that he was in great danger escaped by a back window over the rooftops to make a timely exit from the city.

Surprisingly, it was not until 6.00pm that the two troops of horse soldiers that had been stationed outside the city in preparation for trouble were brought onto the scene. The Alderman and the Town Clerk advocated the immediate use of force to clear the square but the Colonel-in-Charge, Colonel Brereton, strongly disapproved of the use of violence in this case, and ordered his troops to disperse the crowd by slowly and peacefully riding through them. It seemed to do the trick for after talking and handshaking with many of the crowd the Colonel reported that they were in good humour and that he was satisfied that they would soon be going home for the night.

By the next morning Brereton believed that the worst of the violence was over. After the breaches in the Mansion House had been boarded up he ordered the handful of troops left in the Square to be withdrawn. But Brereton had seriously underestimated the depth of discontent for by 8.00am a crowd had again gathered outside the Mansion House. Seizing their chance they stormed the unprotected building. It was now the Mayor's turn to flee for his life across the rooftops.

It was at about this time that a most ill advised and fateful decision was made; the two troops of the 14th Light Dragoons, 'the bloody blues', were ordered to leave the city at a trot. This surprising command was given because the troops were reported to be not only exhausted after a twenty hour period on standby but also it was believed that the Dragoons' reputation for violence was causing more harm than good. Doubtless it was a tactical blunder. The small force of the Third Dragoon – numbering only thirty-three cavalry men – that remained, were powerless by themselves to maintain order; they were left in the position of being merely helpless onlookers. The city was at the mercy of the looters. The withdrawal of the 14th Dragoons was a rioter's charter.

The news of the soldiers' departure spread quickly and soon several buildings were under attack. The gaols were the rioters' first target. The antiquated Bridewell was ransacked within minutes and all the prisoners were freed. Over at the New Gaol, Mr Humphries, the governor, fearing that his prison would be under attack at any moment hurried to the Guild Hall to receive instructions as to whether he should defend the gaol or release the inmates. But officials in the Guild Hall were in such a state of panic that he received no guidance and left announcing that he would use his discretion.

Within minutes of his return a crowd swarmed across Princes Street Bridge and besieged the Gaol. A gaoler who viewed the scene from the roof excitedly, and somewhat inaccurately, shouted down to his colleagues that the prison was surrounded by ten or twelve thousand people. In comparison with the gate of the Bridewell the metal gates of the New Gaol were strong, but not strong enough to resist the continued battering of the crowd. After three quarters of an hour of energetic hammering, accompanied by 'language of a most savage nature', a hole was beaten through the gate. After a couple of people had climbed through, the gates were opened to the mob. Three hundred people surged into the building to liberate the inmates; within minutes the gaol had lost its 170 prisoners.

The mob continued on its wave of violence with drunken gangs marauding through the city unopposed. The Bishop's Palace was raided and the Mansion House, along with other property in Queen Square, set alight.

In the evening a troop of yeomanry from Gloucestershire unexpectedly arrived in Bristol to offer their assistance. Captain Codrington spent two hours riding round the city trying to obtain the permission from various authorities for his troops to be engaged against the rioters. Eventually, he was so exasperated by the confusion that he shouted at Brereton 'This is too bad. I will not be humbugged in this manner any longer,' and rode home.[10]

It was on Monday morning, the third day of the riot, that the troops of the 14th were called back and reinforcements arrived from Gloucester. Order was only restored after much bloodshed. The troops charged through the streets freely slashing with their sabres. In all it has been loosely 'estimated' that between two hundred and fifty and five hundred people died in the disturbances from drunkenness, drowning, fire and the sword.

The riots were, of course, a national topic of discussion and the events added fuel to the already explosive debate over Reform. The anti-reformists saw the riots as a foretaste of the new democracy and claimed that the rioters were madmen bitten by the 'fiery serpent of the press' [11]. In an article on the troubles the anti-reformist *Blackwoods Advertiser* warned that 'there is not a city, town, village or hamlet…where if the restraints of law were removed the mob would not rise up above their superiors.' On a more positive side, however, a pamphlet *Thoughts on Education, Union of Classes and Cooperation suggested by the Late Riots of Bristol* noted that a vast proportion of rioters were unable to read and pressed for the extension of education to lift the working man from a life of 'ignorance, sensuality and vice' to a state of 'knowledge, intellect and virtue.' [12]

Back in Bristol, after the disturbances the Mayor was tried for neglect of duty and Colonel Brereton was court martialed. The Mayor was acquitted, though more on account of sympathy for his frail physique – he was unable to ride a horse – than for his management of the debacle.

At the end of the fourth day of Brereton's trial, the mild mannered Colonel could take the humiliation of his court martial no more. He went home, and without, as was his custom, saying goodnight to his children, shot himself through the head.[13]

A special commission was also set up to try the rioters – eventually four were hanged outside the New Goal and eighty were sentenced to transportation or lesser punishment. Although some of those convicted were hardened troublemakers, there were many who were hitherto honest family men who had unfortunately become carried away by the horrific dynamics of mob violence.

Whatever view is taken of the riot, the Corporation was utterly discredited. That even the law-abiding citizens felt a certain distance from the Corporation is exemplified by the lack of response at the height of the riot to pleas for help. The citizens not only refused to enroll as special constables before Wetherall's arrival but they also withheld their support for the duration of the troubles. In fact, thousands of 'well dressed' onlookers unintentionally protected the rioters by their presence on the street and did nothing to stop the looting that was so brazenly happening under their noses.

In short, a new age was dawning on local government yet the Corporation was still muddling through on an outmoded system of laissez-faire when it should have been offering positive guidelines for the improvement of a rapidly expanding city. The riots were part of the price to be paid by an alienated corporation that had neglected the working person and their changing environment.

(Afterword: The Reform Act was eventually passed in 1832; the King, who felt 'deepest affliction' due to the 'scenes of violence and outrage...which have occurred in the City of Bristol' recommended the establishment of municipal police forces throughout the Kingdom; and finally, in 1835, the Corporation of Bristol was reorganised under the auspices of the Municipal Corporations Reform Act.)

BRUNEL'S BLUNDERS

If the spirit of the Victorian age is symbolised by the railways, then Brunel's Temple Meads station must surely be the era's cathedral. The station's sheer scale and size dwarf any other previous secular buildings in Bristol; not for nothing has it been called 'one of the greatest industrial monuments to the city.' [14]

Temple Meads station was originally built as the terminus for the Great Western Railway, the seeds of which were sown at a meeting of Bristol businessmen in offices at Temple Back in 1833. The railway was established with a capital of £2 million. By the time the line to London opened in July 1841, costs had exceeded £8 million. The chief engineer to oversee the work was Bristol's most famous adopted son, Isambard Kingdom Brunel. Brunel was at the height of his creative energy; his design for Clifton Suspension Bridge had been accepted in 1831, the ss Great Western had been launched in 1837, and the ss Great Britain in 1843. One could travel to Bristol in Brunel's railway, stay in Brunel's Great Western Hotel and sail to America on Brunel's ships. The 'little giant' was master of both the land and sea.

Brunel's station at Temple Meads – built on part of the site of the only recently established cattle market – was in two distinct parts. The front, in tudor castellated style, was built for large offices, the reception of passengers and living accommodation for the station master. Victorian arbiters of taste like Pugin and Ruskin ridiculed the GWR's tudor style as anachronistic and inappropriate; they certainly had a point, but in many

The Temple Meads terminus of the Great Western Railway was opened in July 1841.
(City of Bristol Museum and Art Gallery)

ways, the design, rather than being backward looking is so confident – almost theatrical that it seems a suitable reflection of Victorian ebullience.

Once the tickets had been bought travellers proceeded, surprisingly, upstairs to the railway which was raised up on an arched viaduct. It was all very exciting and dramatic. The engine shed is enormous and even by today's standards the 72 feet span of the mock hammerbeam roof is impressive.

Despite the seemingly obvious advantages of railway transport there were those who objected to its introduction. The landed gentry formed the most vociferous opposition for it was mostly over their land that the railways ran. There were also some more bizarre objections; farmers feared that their sheep would be stained by smutty smoke, whilst in Buckinghamshire it was conjectured that the sight of a GWR train puffing past the playing fields of Eton would stir up thoughts of revolution in the minds of the impressionable pupils.

Nevertheless, these objections were overruled and the Great Western Railway was built. Today Brunel's work is overwhelmingly remembered with respect and affection. But Brunel has not always been held in such reverence. Brunel may have been a man of exciting vision, but, in common with many geniuses, he was also arrogant and unwilling to compromise. His stubbornness, and indeed the way that he would sometimes ignore the practicalities of the matter, did not endear him to everybody. The Mayor of Bristol was to declare that the city was 'waking from its trance' and he foresaw 'the light of better days approaching at railway speed.' This may have been so, but because of Brunel's unfortunate insistence on the use of broad gauge the speed was not so much of an express, but a goods train.

Even with the benefit of hindsight, John Latimer wrote 50 years later that Brunel was 'an inexperienced theorist, enamoured of novelty, prone to seek difficulties rather than evade them, and utterly indifferent to the outlay which his recklessness entailed upon his employers.' [15]

So why the discontent? Brunel had contentiously chosen the 7 feet broad gauge railway for the Great Western line rather than Stephenson's more widely accepted 4 feet 8 inches narrow gauge. The broad gauge's advantage of providing a more comfortable ride in effect threw a barrier round the South West and handicapped Bristol in its competition with the northern ports. It was a remarkable blunder. Usually a man of vision, Brunel seemed unwilling to accept that the rail network would spread across the land, asserting that the GWR would never have any connection with other main lines. He was soon proved wrong. By 1844 it was possible to travel by rail from Bristol as far as Newcastle. The journey was interrupted, however, at Gloucester where it was necessary to change from broad to narrow gauge. Such a change, which was merely an inconvenience for passengers, entailed a good deal of extra labour for freight. The cheapness of railway transport came through its continuity; to lose this and incur the unnecessary loading and unloading of freight increased costs drastically. Because of

Brunel's stubborness Bristol's port and industries were unable to take full advantage of the invention of the age.

There was another problem. 'God's Wonderful Railway' had come so far, yet it stopped a few hundred yards short of what should have been its most useful destination – the docks. It seems almost inconceivable that it was not for another thirty years that a line connected Temple Meads with the port. Eventually, a tunnel was dug under Redcliffe Hill taking a line that ran across the mouth of the Bathurst Basin to Wapping Wharf. It was such an immediate success that ships were soon reluctant to moor anywhere except by the railway. It was consequently decided 'to connect also Bathurst Wharf with the General Railway System; where for want of such accommodation consignees refuse to have their vessels berthed, and sheds now lie idle' [16].

Brunel's blunders aside, 160 years later Bristol can only be grateful to the engineer; to many visitors the Clifton Suspension Bridge, the ss Great Britain and the GWR Terminal epitomise Bristol.

THE DARK SECRETS OF REDCLIFFE CAVES

While building the docks railway in 1861, the navvies tunnelling through Redcliffe Hill uncovered an underground passage; once again, Redcliffe's best known secret had been 'discovered.' For most people living in the vicinity, the unearthing of the passage came as no surprise. Any true Redclivian knew only too well about the caves and the tales of smugglers and slaves attached to them. The railway engineers, however, were keen to find out more and so, in true pioneering spirit, armed with candles and torches and clinging nervously to a rope lest they lost their way, they ventured into the darkness.

'After creeping through a low narrow passage, some twenty yards in length, the party came to a row of arches, each of which led in an opposite direction. Taking the centre one, the party had to crawl on their hands and knees for about ten yards under a great rock, and then they emerged into a spacious and lofty cavern, whence there were other branches. A journey of two or three hundred feet further chiefly through low narrow corridors, brought them to what appeared to be the grand salon or chief cave. It is perfectly circular in form, the room sloping to a few feet off the ground...Although the party explored some six or seven branches most were walled up or filled with rubbish.' [17]

What had happened was that over the years the caves had been used as a rubbish tip. Numerous shafts had been dug from above and all sorts of detritus deposited down them. The Shot Tower had made use of such shafts for dumping ashes that were then carried away by wheelbarrow to far-off corners. Excavations in 1938 and 1939 also revealed great piles of pottery and glass. So, with all this spoil, and also because several of the chambers are walled up, the caves have retained some of their secrets and even today their full extent remains unsurveyed.[18]

The caves are man-made; in some places there can still be seen the marks of the hatchets used in their excavation. But why was this network of caves dug? The answer is tantalisingly simple. Sand may be the world's most common mineral, but it is still highly prized, especially when the source is within a city. The uses of sand and sandstone are almost limitless and would have been used for building, repairing roads, glass industry – it was particularly suitable for the production of heavy bottle glass – and as a glaze for the local coarse pottery. And it also played an important part in Bristol's maritime trade, indeed Redcliffe's sandstone is said to be spread round the ports of the world because of its use as ballast. It was written in 1657, of one ship that the 'Ballist that was then on board was good clift Ballist and such Ballast as ships of this port of Bristoll doe usually carry to Virginia.' [19] As to the age of the caves, although the earliest written reference appears in the sixteenth century they must be much older – some parts of the excavations are probably as old as the Southern Parishes themselves.

Caves are invariably imbued with dark secrets and mysteries and this warren of chambers is no exception. Across the country stories of caves and smugglers seem to go hand in hand. What are caves for, if not to be used as a warehouse for contraband? Unfortunately for storytellers any such tales about Redcliffe Caves are certainly spurious – so obvious a hiding place would have defeated its own purpose.

Local folklore also links Redcliffe Caves with Bristol's slave trade. Shackles are reputed to have been found in the caves, but are unlikely to be anything to do with slaves. The few slaves that did come to Bristol were far too valuable to be kept in such dark and dank surroundings.

Prisoners of war, however, were another matter – and this is the more likely origin of the shackles. From 1654, when Cromwell ordered that Bristol's Norman castle be demolished, the city had no secure place for the detention of foreign prisoners. In 1665 the situation became so desperate that fifty Dutch prisoners, captured by Admiral Blake and Vice Admiral Penn, were brought to Redcliffe and lodged, of all places, in the crypt of the church, where they stayed for over four months before being transported to more suitable accommodation at Chepstow Castle.[20]

The difficulties of prisoner-of-war accommodation arose again a century later when wars raged on the continent. Consequently a Mr French offered his one-acre yard as a makeshift detention centre. Records of Mr French's prison – on a site at the rear of the present day General Hospital (a French's lane still runs off Guinea Street) are scant and disjointed but they do seem to indicate that his yard was connected by a passage to the caves. Spanish prisoners were kept in this passage in 1741 and it was again used for French prisoners in 1744.[21]

The security in French's yard was lax. It was bounded by a nine-foot high wall, but even when prisoners escaped where were they to go? Apart from stowing away on a ship foreign prisoners were unlikely to get far. Nevertheless there were escapes. On one occasion a group of Spaniards who had been given leave to wash their linen failed to return[22] while in January 1745 it was reported that 'a number of men attempted to escape by scaling a wall in Guinea Street; one being shot dead by the sentinel, the others retreated to their prison in the rock.'[23] Despite this breach, in March of the same year another '175 men were landed at the Key, and from there conveyed to Redcliffe Hill where they were immediately put under proper confinement.'[24] The yard continued in occasional use, but after an outbreak of typhus in 1780 it was abandoned, and the prisoners transferred to a less crowded spot at Knowle.

Over the following years the caves gradually slipped out of public notice, being used for the more mundane purposes of pottery store and, of course, rubbish tip. Until, that is, the railway navvies hacked their way through what was probably the very passage that led to French's Yard.

In the Second World War the caves were in the news again when they were used for air raid shelters. How safe they were is open to conjecture for when bombs demolished Redcliffe Infants' School a crater penetrated right down into the caverns below.

And what of the Redcliffe caves today? At the time of writing the caves are closed to the public while the City Council ponders developments on Alfred's Wharf. Hopefully, in the not too distant future, the caves will once more be open for regular guided tours – they are certainly a fascinating and mysterious link with Bristol's past.

Notes
1.	J. Lord & J. Southam, *The Floating Harbour* (Redcliffe Press, 1983) p.34
2.	Felix Farley's *Bristol Journal* April 29th, 1809
3.	Felix Farley's *Bristol Journal* May 13th, 1809
4.	J. Latimer, *Annals of Bristol in the 18th Century* (Bristol, 1893) p.407
5.	L. Vear, *South of the Avon* (Wotton-Under-Edge, 1978) p.120
6.	*Report of the Visiting Justices into the Gaol and Bridewell of the City of Bristol* (1841) p.5
7.	Ibid p.9
8.	*Morning Chronicle* (London, January 4th, 1832)
9.	W. H. Somerton, *Report of the Trials* (Bristol, 1832) p.77
10.	G. Amey, *City Under Fire* (Guildford and London, 1979) p.78
11.	Blackwoods Advertiser, *What Caused the Bristol Riots* (1832) p.474
12.	Thoughts on Education, *Union of Classes and Cooperation suggested by the Late Riots of Bristol* (London.1831) p.10
13.	P. MacDonald, *Hotheads and Heroes* (Swansea, 1986) p.129
14.	R. A. Buchanan, *Industrial Archaeology of Bristol* (1967) p.15
15.	John Latimer, *Annals of Bristol in the 19th Century* (Bristol, 1887) p.191
16.	J. Lord & J. Southam, op. cit, p.76
17.	A Birmingham newspaper dated October 24th, 1868
18.	In the mid 1980s the Temple Local History Group undertook a thorough survey of the accessible parts of the cave system. Ed. Julian Lea-Jones, *Bristol Past Revisited* (Temple Local History Group,1989) p.21-27.
19.	P. McGrath, *Merchants and Merchandise in 17th Century,* (Bristol, 1955) p.247
20.	J. F. Nichols & J. Taylor, *Bristol Past and Present* (Bristol, 1881) Vol 2, p.22
21.	J. C. Whining, *Redcliffe Caves,* unpublished manuscript Bristol Central Reference Library B243811p.26
22.	Margaret Franklin, *Prisoners of War in Bristol* – extracts from Public Record Office Greenwich, unpublished manuscript, Bristol Central Reference Library B30152
23.	J. C. Whining, op cit, p.26
24.	*Bristol Oracle and County Intelligencer* March 9th, 1745

Other Sources:
R. A. Buchanan & M. Williams, *Brunel's Bristol,* (Redcliffe Press, 1982). C. Crick, *Victorian Buildings in Bristol,* (Redcliffe Press, 1975). F. Greenacre and S. Stoddard, *The Bristol Landscape* (Bristol, 1986). A. Gomme, M. Jenner, B. Little, *Bristol, An Architectural History* (Bristol 1979). R. Waiters, *The Establishment of the Bristol Police Force* (1975).

View from Welsh Back looking toward Redcliffe Back and St Mary Redcliffe. The Floating Harbour was not just unpleasant to smell but was a risk to health. (City of Bristol Museum and Art Gallery)

SIX

PUBLIC HEALTH

Indian Cholera first appeared in the northern coal ports and spread across England reaching Bristol in the summer of 1831. The disease mostly struck in those areas that were the least salubrious; in Bristol, the finger of death pointed first to the desperately overcrowded St Peter's Workhouse and then to the parishes of Redcliffe, Temple and St Thomas. To many people, even in an age when the nature of disease was not understood, it came as no surprise. There was an innate feeling that the filthy, overcrowded condition of the parishes constituted a time bomb that would eventually claim many lives. By the beginning of the nineteenth century the golden age of the Southern Parishes had become severely tarnished.

Of course, the parishes had always had a boisterous feel about them. Sailors crammed into the inns, taverns and boarding houses spending their wages, or making the most of what Bristol could offer before they set off on voyages that could last months, or even years. When Revd. Thomas Clarkson gathered evidence in 1787 for Wilberforce on the evils of the slave trade he made straight for the low-life of the Southern Parishes. Clarkson's brief was to see how the trade corrupted those who took part in it. To this end, with a face blackened like a miner, he hung around such pubs as the Seven Stars just off St Thomas Street. He heard plenty of talk about atrocities. For many sailors, life was nasty, brutish and often short. This had always been so. Yet the difference now was that the very fabric of the Southern Parishes, the buildings, the sanitation and the roads, was overstretched and overburdened. Redcliffe, Temple and St Thomas were so teeming with life that they seemed to be bursting at the seams. The decline is evident as early as 1813 when a guide book to Bristol warned visitors of the perils that could be encountered on a visit to St Mary Redcliffe:

'The usual approach is by a long narrow street (Redcliffe Street) skirted by small shops and from its contracted nature and its peculiarity of position is generally dirty, black and perilous to the passenger, several manufactories, warehouses and workshops of not the most pleasant and odoriferous kind are distributed on the left and the right whilst the narrow thoroughfare is generally crowded by colliers, sandmen, sledges, sailors, asses and carts.'

The writer concluded by emphasising that:

'In such a situation personal safety is the first care.'

Mathews' Guide of 1815 also warned of something that was as much a concern to the residents as it was to genteel visitors: the 'most noxious pestilential filth' of the harbour:

'Every care is taken by the Dock-company to prevent all unwholesome exhalations: though in strict justice it must be acknowledged, that in opposition to all truely laudable exertions, in the summer season particularly, the water acquires a dark unpleasant surface; and where it is most subject to the reception of drains emits a rather offensive smell'. [1]

Simply, the foul smell of the floating harbour arose from the six miles of sewers draining into it. In the old days the odour had been bearable for the harbour had been cleaned twice daily by the tides. But now, with the slower circulation of the water because of the Float the nuisance was becoming intolerable. The float was not just unpleasant to smell, it was also a health risk.

Despite what the editor of *Mathews' Guide* had written, it was a problem that the Dock Company resolutely ignored. Even though it was undoubtedly their responsibility, the directors felt under no obligation to help. Eventually in the hot summer of 1825 the company's stubborn refusal to cooperate led to a writ being issued against them. The dock company was at last ordered to make whatever alterations were necessary to clear the Float of sewage.

When the poor were ill or suffering poverty beyond endurance, they could as a last resort enter St Peter's Poorhouse. St Peter's, which was across the water from our parishes, had been a poorhouse in one form or another since 1697 when the parishes of Bristol were grouped together to form a co-operative system of relief. Although the half timbered medieval building was maintained as well as conditions allowed, it was dreadfully crowded with up to six hundred inhabitants at any one time. So, not surprisingly, when the 1831 epidemic of cholera swept the country it was a primary target for the disease. Of two hundred and sixty-one cases reported in the city, one hundred and sixty-eight occurred in St Peter's.

On just one day at the peak of the epidemic, thirty-one victims of the disease were ferried across the river and buried in Temple churchyard. Because the numbers were so high a bizarre rumour spread that paupers were being buried alive just to get rid of them. There followed a macabre scene in the churchyard where members of a crowd exhumed some of the recently buried bodies so as to be sure that they were truly dead.

Even before the cholera outbreak it had been obvious that the medical facilities in Bristol were overstretched and that a new hospital was needed to supplement the work of the Bristol Infirmary (established 1737). With this in mind a group – many of whom

*'Vermin Farm' in the shadow of Redcliffe Church – a warren of dirty
rotten sheds rumoured to be a haven for criminals.
(City of Bristol Museum and Art Gallery)*

were Quakers – got together to promote the establishment of the Bristol General Hospital. With the cholera outbreak, the Bristol riots and general state of national unrest because of the Reform Bill, 1831 was hardly an auspicious year for new ventures. Nevertheless, after a survey of sites in the city, suitable premises were found in Guinea Street, in accommodation already owned by Dr Kentish.

The situation, by Bathurst Basin and The Cut was described as airy and was well placed for the growing populations of South Bristol and Bedminster. There was one objection, however - its closeness to Acraman's Anchor Works. Concern was expressed that the constant hammering and clattering from the forge – as well as the fumes – would have a far from recuperative effect on the patients. A sub committee appointed to look into this reported that any such fears were unfounded and furthermore declared the site to be 'particularly salubrious and desirable.' 2

After a slight delay over the appointment of staff due to 'the disturbed state of public affairs' the hospital was formally opened on November 1st, 1832. From the beginning the twenty beds were well used; indeed with up to 40 in-patients being looked after at any one time, beds frequently had to be shared. Even though there was still no understanding of bacteria or anaesthetics the patients were at least well fed. The meals provided were:

'Breakfast-6ozs. of bread. 1 pint of tea.
Dinner-6ozs. of meat and potatoes, four days a week. 1 quart of broth, and 12 ozs. of
boiled rice on other days. 1 Pint of beer.
Supper-6ozs. of bread. 1 pint of gruel .' 3

Doctors were trained to as high a standard as medical knowledge would allow, but in the days before Florence Nightingale the quality of nursing was not high. The matron's job was said to be particularly demanding - so much so that she requested a supply of beer to steady her nerves: 'The matron finds it necessary for her health to use a little porter', the hospital committee were told. Accordingly they ordered three dozen pint bottles for the matron's use.4

Acramans was finally silenced in 1851 when the General Hospital bought the works for further development. In its early days the hospital led a hand-to-mouth existence but by the 1850s finances were on a sure enough footing for new purpose built premises to be planned. Two four-storey blocks were built – one facing the New Cut, the other the Bathurst Basin. Compared with the rudimentary Guinea Street premises the new hospital was a showpiece. There was a bathroom with hot and cold water on each floor, a steam driven lift, speaking tubes and even heating in the passageways.5 Another novel feature of the hospital was that the ground floor was designed and let out as a warehouse. It was hoped that the prime warehouse space so close to Bathurst Basin would generate extra income for the hospital.

Although the terrible mortality of 1831 caused some to wonder if cholera was connected to the unsanitary conditions of the large towns, Parliament did not consider

*Three Kings Inn, St Thomas Street. The community had grown rotten with old age,
the houses had decayed as had the reputation of their inhabitants.
(City of Bristol Museum and Art Gallery)*

the matter seriously until 1840. An enquiry in 1840 into the public health of towns was a pioneering initiative. For the first time it showed an awareness of the need for statutory control in planning the future of the nation's rapidly expanding towns and cities (though how seriously this was taken at a local level was another matter). The national commission of 1840 was followed in 1844 by local enquiries into public health and predictably the picture that was drawn of Bristol's dark and reeking streets was most unflattering.

Commissioner Sir Henry De La Beche found conditions so unpleasant during one of his tours of Bristol's slums that he hastily disappeared down an alley to vomit. Even the strong stomach of the Government was turned by what it saw.[6]

The report announced that the mortality rate in Bristol was scandalously high - at thirty-one in every thousand, it was exceeded only by two other areas in England. To the commissioners the cause of this high rate was obvious: the lack of sewerage in many parts of Bristol. They wrote:

'Viewed as a sanitary question there are few if any large towns in England in which the supply of water is so inadequate as Bristol.' [7]

The Parishes of Redcliffe, Temple and St Thomas were singled out as having the worst conditions. The parishes not only had a growing population in an already over crowded area but moreover the water supply was insufficient and sometimes unreliable. Everybody depended on the communal taps and ancient conduits for their 'fresh water.' No house in any of the three parishes had its own water supply. Sometimes in the summer months even the minimal supplies would fail and parishioners had to buy water by the jar for the exorbitant price of a halfpenny or three-farthings. The opinion of the commissioners was that:

'As the climate is salubrious and poverty not particularly severe we can only look for the causes of the unhealthy state of the city in the neglect of the proper sanitary conditions. We have seen these to be bad drainage and sewerage, deficient supplies of water, bad structural arrangements of streets and dwellings and an overcrowded population.' [8]

The report optimistically concluded:

'These are in great measure removable causes and most of them are within the recognizable province of legislation.' [9]

At a time when the mere hint of guidance from central government gave rise to fears of 'centralisation' and 'interference', the commissioners' faith in legislation was unjustified. Little was done to remedy the unhealthy conditions.

With monotonous predictability yet another epidemic was soon to rage through Bristol. The outbreak of cholera in the city in 1849 claimed 444 lives in just four weeks. The outbreak even swept through the previously salubrious Redcliffe Parade, a row of houses on a high and airy situation overlooking the docks. It did, however, nudge a few councillors into action and another inquiry was initiated. Once more the conditions of the three Southern Parishes were brought to the forefront and described as shocking in every detail. Bristol's great historian John Latimer omitted the details from his *Annals of Bristol* explaining that:

'no conception of the actual facts could be given without employing terms repugnant to modern habits and good taste.' [10]

According to the police there were a hundred and thirty-two grimy, overcrowded courts in the parishes of Redcliffe, Temple and St Thomas some of which were never visited by the scavenger (refuse collector). With few restrictions on what owners could do with their property, landlords utilised every inch by cramming dwellings into any little space available. Yards and gardens were built over, passages and landings colonised and even windowless cabins constructed. Little consideration was given to sanitation. Typical was Nelson Place, a row of sixteen tiny hovels behind Redcliffe Parade, which was without drainage. The privies at the rear of the houses were emptied only every three or four years, the contents being dumped into a hole in the small front garden.

The Southern Parishes had turned into a human warren of dirty rotten sheds, and because of the anonymity that they offered it was rumoured to be a haven for criminals. In the crowded Queens Head Court, there was a slaughter-house: 'a very objectionable place with pig stye, stable and manure heap all under cover.' The Dean of the Cathedral described in the report a Dickensian underworld of 'squalid dwelling places 'which demoralised the population into a life of vice maddened with lust, drunkenness and violence.' The Dean saw the people as morally contaminated by their surroundings and asked:

'How can the inhabitants be decent and orderly when they are compelled to live by day and night in rooms crowded with persons, many of them of the most abandoned character, from the sight of whose disgusting habits and the hearing of whose blasphemous words they have no escape?' [11]

But the picture gets even worse, for not only were the living crowded together but so also were the dead. Although the Arnos Vale cemetery had been opened in 1838 its use was only slowly adopted. The graveyards in the Southern Parishes were described as full, yet in St Mary Redcliffe's churchyard, for example, there were still on average 146 internments a year. The churchyards of St Thomas was so full that there were bones strewn over the ground whilst at other churchyard the smell of decay invaded nearby houses.

Conditions were so undeniably bad that this time the Council took heed of the report and set up a Sanitary Authority. At last things began to happen: in the next fifteen years a most impressive drainage system was installed throughout the city and, moreover, by 1866 it was claimed that nearly every house was connected to the mains water supply. On a less dramatic scale an Inspector of Nuisances diligently went about his work closing down illegal slaughterhouses, isolating fever cases and providing an efficient scavenging service. The courts were now visited almost daily and large iron bins were provided for household refuse.

Although Bristol as a whole was becoming a cleaner and healthier place in which to live there was still little room for complacency. For the problems of Redcliffe, Temple and St Thomas these measures were merely a palliative – the over-crowded slum dwellings, the winding, crooked passages of the Southern Parishes needed an altogether stronger medicine.

HUNGER HAUNTED HOMES

Like many other cities in the Victorian period, Bristol grew at a phenomenal rate. During Queen Victoria's reign, the city virtually quadrupled in area whilst the population which in 1869 amounted to 190,000 had by 1901 nearly doubled to 365,000. Villages such as Brislington, Bedminster and Knowle which not long before had been in the clean air of the countryside were swallowed up.

The physical growth of Bristol was due both to an expansion of population and to an exodus of middle and artisan classes from the older, central parishes. The middle classes moved into spacious suburban houses in the tree-lined streets of Clifton, Redland, Cotham, St Andrews and Knowle, whilst many artisans moved into new accommodation especially to the east and south of the city. Such moves were not always a change for the better and it was warned in 1908 that 'whole areas of the suburbs are arising which from lack of any definite policy will soon become little better than slums.'

With so much building going on around them, the older parishes of the city were left becalmed like the vortex of a hurricane. The parishes of Redcliffe, Temple and St Thomas soon found they housed a disproportionate number of sick, elderly and other generally disadvantaged people, in other words, all those who had little opportunity to move to the new Eden of the suburbs. This does not mean the parishes emptied. Far from it, for it was in this area that many of Bristol's biggest employers were based, so that accommodation for people working locally was at a premium. Between 1801 and 1841 the population of Redcliffe, Temple and St Thomas had increased by over fifty per cent – from 9,042 to 14,617. Every house was crowded and because of high demand, accommodation was by no means cheap.

Some of the worst dwellings were squashed round the base of St Mary Redcliffe forming a notorious 'red light' area (being a port there was never a lack of demand for prostitutes) known to the police as Vermin Farm. Here, it was not unknown for eight to ten people to sleep in one room. And similar tales are told of Temple Parish where poverty and pauperism were said to be indigenous. Temple was reputed to be a haunt of thieves; the crowded alleys, the low cavernous courts and the narrow lanes were accredited with sheltering marauders who spent their nights plundering the city only to return at daybreak to catch a few hours' sleep before they 'hasten to get drunk – the business of the day.'

The shocking fact was that much of this slum dwelling belonged to the church. The St Mary Redcliffe Vestry had made the mistake of leasing houses to unscrupulous people who for years were entrusted with the control of the dwellings. Unfortunately, when many of these leases had expired the church found that their property had declined into slum dwellings.

There had been some improvements. One weekly event that had not helped the state of the streets was the Thomas Street market that had been initiated way back in 1570. By now it was largely for horses, cattle and pigs. In 1829 it was transferred to the less populous Temple Meads.

Ten years later another long standing tradition, the Temple Street Fair, came to an end. Held at the beginning of March it was an important trading event bringing together hawkers of produce from all over the country. For nine days Temple Street was crowded with colourful stalls; with hardware from Sheffield and Birmingham, lace from Nottingham, millinery, haberdashery and trinkets from London and a wide amount of local produce including everything to do with woollen manufacture – cloths, carpets, rugs, blankets, linen, and a remarkable selection of buck, doe and hog-skins for breeches. There was also a great show of cattle and horses and a variety of sideshows, exhibitions and entertainments.

But as the years went by, it appeared that the places of trade were diminishing while the number of shows, entertainments and general disorder increased. Amongst other things *Mathew's Bristol Guide* of 1815 listed: 'Exhibitions of Wild Beasts and Birds, Wax-works, Wire-dancing, Tumbling, Balancing, Puppets, Punch with his wife Joan, Seafights, Conjuration, Magic and Mummery of all sorts.' Alcohol was sold at a number of unlicensed premises and by the 1830s the fair was said to be a centre of corruption and demoralisation, attracting an increasing number of thieves, pickpockets and swindlers. A quick-eyed councillor reported that on one night he had counted no fewer than two hundred and twenty thieves and prostitutes loitering about. A committee consequently appointed to investigate the fair recommended its suppression, 'thereby preventing a re-occurrence of those disgusting scenes of profaneness, of drunkeness and debauchery which invariably and to an alarming extent prevailed.' [12]

The suppression of Temple Fair can be seen as a reflection of the formation at the beginning of the Victorian era of a new set of values. The Bristol Tee-Total Society had been established in 1836 and a year later boasted over 1,000 members. Previous social reformers had been content to denounce only alcoholic spirits, recognising beer as a cheap and wholesome drink greatly preferable to impure water. But to the new temperance movement even beer threatened the realization of the Victorian dream: the secure home, family life, sobriety, Christianity and happiness. This fad for abstinence was all very well for the middle classes in their comfortable homes. For the down-trodden slum dwellers of the inner cities, alcohol was still an important escape. Indeed, in these quarters the drinking man was so respected that the tobacco manufacturer W.D. Wills is reported to have lost his seat in Parliament because of a dastardly last minute notice which circulated before election time amongst the ward's publicans that he was an unrepentant tee-totaller.

Improvements in the environment also came about through the benevolence of individuals. In 1829 a wealthy citizen, Mr Weare, had donated £10,000, subject to an annuity of £500, that made way for a widespread series of developments. Thus in 1839 a plan was initiated to widen some of the narrow streets, and create new ones where this would not suffice. Money was also set aside for something that today we take for granted: the naming of streets and the numbering of houses.

Priority was given to the plans to widen Redcliffe Street and lower the tortuous Redcliffe Hill which became impassable due to mud in the winter and wet weather. Nearby, a new street, Phippen Street, was to be built through part of the Vermin Farm locality. By the 1880s the renovations were such in this area that one man was quoted in the *Bristol Mercury* as saying:

'Pile Street, Sir; Why its the Mall - Clifton itself-compared to what it was in the old days before the worst courts were swept away.'[13]

And alongside these improvements the moral tenor of the area was to be improved. It was proposed that a maximum fine of £2 be imposed on anyone committing a nuisance - a term that included soliciting for prostitution.

Such positive plans reflected a refreshing change of attitude for a council renowned for its indifference to environmental problems. But such enlightenment was not widespread. When the council submitted its proposals for comment to the local parishes no replies were received. Pressure did, however, come from other areas, namely local businessmen.

The increase in the speed of travel offered by the change from stage coach to train was quite remarkable. Indeed by 1850 railways had reached a stage not seriously improved upon until the abandonment of steam in the mid twentieth century.

Although the railways opened up communications nationally, on the local roads they indirectly wrought havoc. Because of the concentration of industry to the north of Temple Meads station, and the consequent coming and going of carts, wagons and workers, the streets were becoming stiflingly crowded. It is interesting, and somewhat

*The corner of Redcliffe Street and St Thomas Street prior to demolition
making way for the building of Victoria Street in the 1870s.
ES and A Robinson's original premises at 2 Redcliffe Street.*

paradoxical, that the railways far from being the death knell of horse transport actually encouraged it. In contrast to the declining number of coach horses (prior to the railway there were twenty two coaches daily between London and Bristol - within three months of its introduction they had all stopped) the number of dray and cab horses actually increased. One had only to look at the number of carts loading, unloading and waiting at a factory like Finzel's where 1,800 tons of sugar a week was produced, to realise this.

In the mostly medieval streets of Redcliffe, Temple and St Thomas such an upsurge in road use was a constant source of discontent. The route from Temple Meads Station to Bristol Bridge was circuitous, narrow, dangerous and more to the point, unprestigious – it did nothing to project the modern image the city fathers wanted of Brunel's metropolis. Consequently, in 1846, a report was issued strongly condemning the streets of Temple Parish and recommending that a new street, Victoria Street, should cut a swath through the area. As always, funding was a problem and the city had to wait until 1870 before its new commercial thoroughfare was built. Similarly, Redcliffe Street, Bristol's main artery for traffic to and from Somerset, was broadened from ten to twenty feet between 1875 and 1877. Likewise a scheme to widen Bristol Bridge was completed in 1873. A second bridge, the Half Penny bridge, had already been built across the Avon linking Temple Back with St Phillips in 1838. 'Everything in Redcliffe following the widening of the thoroughfare takes on a far bigger scale than in olden days' wrote the *Bristol Mercury* in 1884.[14] As we shall soon see, with the widening of the roads the full potential of the area's industries could now be unleashed. Yet again a revolution in communications was to enable widespread industrial change.

It should not be thought that these inner city problems were peculiar to Bristol. At a time when Britain was celebrating fifty glorious years of Victoria's reign it was becoming apparent that there was a reservoir of poverty, destitution and crime at the base of this so-called rich and civilised society. Although per capita income had increased substantially the rich benefitted more than the poor. These problems were soon to be given national publicity by such mild mannered men – not revolutionaries – as William Booth and Seebohm Rowntree. William Booth's survey in London, which was echoed by Rowntree's investigations in York, presented the unpalatable view that thirty per cent of the capital's population were living at a level below which they could adequately be fed, housed and clothed.

Remarkably enough, on a lesser scale, Bristol had its own social activist in the form of the campaigning journalist James Crosby, chief reporter of the *Bristol Mercury*. In 1883, five years before Booth's London portrayal, the *Bristol Mercury* launched a survey of the city's poor. The study was notable not only for its compassion but also its relative restraint – a rare feat for high-flown Victorian journalism. Crosby examined some of the rundown parishes of Bristol and talked to the inhabitants. The following report of a conversation with an old Redclivian is typical of what was published:

We had an interesting conversation with an engine fitter of 60 years of age who was at the Avonside works seven years. He is out of work and has brought up a family of six and now has two children under the age of 14. He is a merry minded man who says he is able to work "in the shape of strength but not in the strength of eyes" as he is obliged to wear spectacles and his employers did not think he could do much with spectacles...He used to get 34 shillings to £2 a week and now receives nine shillings a week from his society but that is not enough to live on. He would not live in this dull hole if he could help it. He pays five shillings a week for his house including an old fashioned roomy low roofed kitchen with many signs of comfort but he is "obliged to light the lamp sometimes to see if the fire is burning" and where there is no light there cannot be a lot of health as "light and fresh air are as essential as victuals." No one ought to be "stived up like this" and he thinks Sir ———— has a much better place for his horses.' [15]

For many of the older people the rapid growth of the city had been traumatic. The countryside was no longer a stone's throw away and the days when a young poet like Chatterton or Coleridge could disappear into the fields adjacent to our parishes were long gone.

'One of them complained that "she could not step into the fields like she used to in her younger days – a few hundred yards from her house." She only had to go out of the big gate and up Redcli' Mead Lane and there she was "in the fields at the top." She remembers the time when there was a large tree still growing in the middle of Avon Street, and when the larger houses were inhabited by wealthy traders and merchants. This old lady had lived 95 years and brought up a family of twelve children.'[16]

The *Mercury* took note of recent developments and concurred that there had been much improvement of late. Extended compulsory education and street improvements had done a great work in Redcliffe in the past two decades. The improvements of Redcliffe and Pile Streets had swept away some of the 'foulest dens in the city' whilst the church had done much with the slum property that had been returned to them. Indeed model houses were being built on Redcliffe Hill where they were sacrificing three of the old homes for just one of the new dwellings. However, the *Mercury* went on to say that although the parish of Temple benefitted greatly from the construction of Victoria Street many problems remained: 'the brand new thoroughfare of Victoria Street literally put a new face on Temple – but behind this mask are still the old tumbledown houses.' As they so graphically put it 'a large part of the parish seems to be faithfully following in the footsteps of the church and leaning too.' [17]

Notes

1. *Mathew's Bristol Directory* (Bristol, 1815) p.5
2. J. Odery-Symes, *A Short History of the Bristol General Hospital* (Bristol, 1932) p.4
3. J. Odery-Symes, op cit, p.20
4. ibid, p.21
5. C. Crick, *Victorian Buildings in Bristol* (Redcliffe Press, 1975) p.35
6. D. Large & F. Round, *Public Health in Mid Victorian Bristol* (Bristol, 1974) p.3
7. *Royal Commission on the Health of Towns* (1845) 2nd Report, Appendix on Bristol p.71
8. ibid, p.75
9. ibid, p.75
10. J. Latimer, *Annals of Bristol in the Nineteenth Century* p.313
11. *Report to the General Board of Health on the City and County of Bristol* (1850) p.48
12. G. Bush, *Bristol and its Municipal Government 1820-1851* (Bristol, 1976) p.162
13. *'Homes of the Bristol Poor'*, by the Special Commissioner of the *Bristol Mercury* (Bristol, 1884) p.70
14. ibid, p.67
15. ibid, p.67
16. ibid, p.58
17. ibid, p.58

Other Sources
J. H. Bettey, *Bristol Observed* (Redcliffe Press, 1986)

SEVEN

VICTORIAN INDUSTRIAL ENTERPRISE

For many Bristol historians the nineteenth century, in comparison with previous times, was a period of economic inertia. Certainly Bristol had its problems; it had long ago lost its cherished status of the realm's second city and it lagged behind the fantastic development of Liverpool, Manchester and Birmingham. But in real terms it was hardly stagnant. As we have seen, the population doubled between 1851 and 1901 and also there were some conspicuous examples of industrial success. Unfortunately Bristol's problems, which centred to a large extent on the decline of its docks, have detracted from its successes. One should realise, however, that by the 1870s companies like Fry's, the Great Western Cotton Mills at Barton Hill and the Bristol Wagon Works at Lawrence Hill (also with a large and handsome showroom in Victoria Street) each employed upwards of 900 workers and there were many more firms with employees totalling over 500. Victorian industrial enterprise had not bypassed Bristol.

Despite Brunel's self-inflicted wounds on the Great Western Railway, the railway's development was the very keynote to much of the industrial expansion. Mass production depended on the railways – our local industries could not have done without them. It is therefore not a coincidence that within half a mile of the new Temple Meads Station several companies were growing at a rate undreamed of a few years before. Of the many firms clustered in the loop of the Avon that encompassed the parishes of Redcliffe, Temple and St Thomas perhaps Finzel's Sugar Refinery, Messrs ES & A Robinson and WD & HO Wills stand out as the industrial giants. Their products may have been dissimilar, but their style of management, their interest in technology and their commercial cunning ranked them amongst the best of Bristol's industry.

The Finzel Refinery, which by the 1870s was the largest of its kind in England, was based at the Counterslip, on part of the site until recently occupied by Courage's Brewery. It was founded in 1836 by Conrad Finzel, a German by birth who had been a refugee from Napoleon's army. 'The Good Conrad Finzel', as he was called by many, was a benevolent man. He was reputed to give at least £10,000 a year to Muller's Orphanage at Ashley Down and was also generous to his workforce who were paid more than anyone else in the country doing a similar job. The social relations between Finzel and his workforce were described as 'liberality on the one hand and appreciation on the other.'[1]

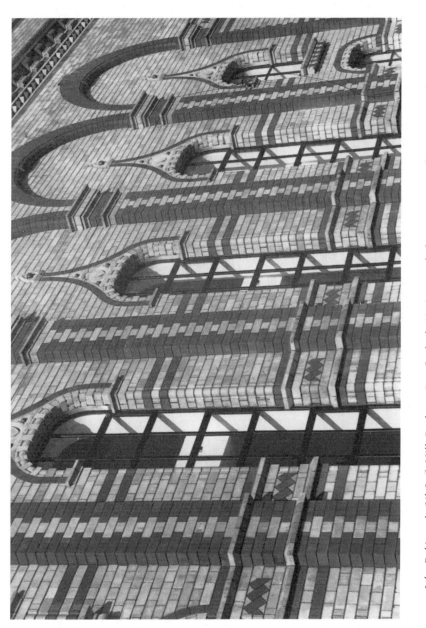

John Robinson's Oil Seed Mill, Bathurst Parade, built 1874. Typical of Victorian Bristol Byzantine architecture. Now restored and a facade for housing. (Photo M. Manson)

Finzel's success came from his invention of the centrifugal process – a process that enabled him to be the first person to manufacture granulated white sugar. Prior to this, all sugar had to be dried slowly in loaves, or baked, creating a somewhat inferior product. With Finzel's invention, however, treated sugar was put into a spin dryer and revolved at a remarkable 500 revolutions a minute, producing after two minutes sugar of 'a pure and colourless appearance.'[2]

Although the factory suffered an almost disastrous setback in 1846 when it was entirely destroyed by fire, by 1873 the firm employed 700 people and had an output of 1,800 tons of sugar a week.[3] The amount of raw material consumed was staggering. Merely to provide power for the operation, 1,000 tons of coal were delivered weekly by barge to the factory.

'There is something stupendous,' wrote the *Practical Magazine* in 1873, 'about the appearance of the street area in front of the building, where drays constantly come and go, and along the tramways at the entrance a continuous stream of raw sugar in boxes, bags and hogsheads are going in, whilst an endless succession of tierces, bags and packages coming out is like the double procession of bees in a mighty hive.'[4]

And once inside the factory the view was equally impressive:

'Some indication of the extent of the works is afforded to the visitor, who having passed through various general offices, cashiers departments, the sale rooms and the sampling room where raw sugars are inspected and purchased, is asked to inspect the engine house and the boiler house...In order to see it properly we must ascend a spiral staircase through the very core of the building, where amidst a prevailing sense of stickyness and a general impression that we are taking in saccharine through the pores, we peer through long dim vistas amidst beams and apertures where the immense series of filtering cylinders are reached only by devious galleries and footways.'[5]

Although the reporter was certainly inspired by what he saw there was one sour note amongst all this sweetness, for 'the recent enormous increase in the price of coal makes a very serious loss to the firm, who have not however raised their quotations for sugar.' A recent reduction of duty on sugar had enabled Finzels to keep their prices stable – but only just.

Another of Bristol's staple imports was tobacco. The great family-run tobacco firm of Wills had moved from Castle Street in 1791 to a triple-gabled, ramshackle building in Redcliffe Street. The firm puffed along at an unremarkable rate producing snuff and pipe tobacco until 1861, when with the introduction of a steam engine, business expanded so rapidly that by the end of the decade new premises were needed again.

It was in the 1870s that smoking cigarettes became popular and in the next few years Wills was to become a household name not only in Britain but throughout the Empire.

The introduction of the cigarette allowed women to sample tobacco with somewhat less stigma being attached to what had previously been considered an unfeminine habit.

In 1890 H.H Wills contentiously announced that smoking is a matter that every English woman must settle in her own conscience, and if she is married she must settle it between herself and her husband. [7]

The fine new Wills factory built in Redcliffe Street in 1869 was not merely utilitarian, it was also an impressive monument to Victorian industriousness. Designed by the architects of Bristol's Grand Hotel, Foster and Wood, its facade was of a similar flamboyant renaissance style. Inside, the factory contained not only the most modern machinery but also, for the convenience of the management, a passenger lift. Every floor had toilets and washrooms and there was a library 'to which all have access.' Indeed, for some, conditions at work were probably healthier than those at home.

'Instead of having to mount stairs innumerable, the aid of a friendly lift is called. A bell is sounded, and almost in less than no time down comes the machinery with its attendant: the visitor takes his place alongside his guide and in a twinkling he finds himself at the top of the building . . . This part of the manufactory faces Redcliffe Backs, and here the trollies land the hogsheads, tierces and bales in which the leaves are packed. By means of a hoist they are hauled up to the top of the five storey building...' [8]

As with many other Bristol factories both men and women were employed, though departments were usually segregated by sex (sometimes boys would work alongside women). Thus, in Wills, the sorting of tobacco was done by women, the cutting by men and then it was the women again who did the packing into tins. An enthusiastic reporter from the *Bristol Times and Mercury* was most impressed by the quality of the Wills workforce numbering about 500 in the Redcliffe Street factory in 1883 and wrote:

'Looking at these trim tidy girls with their smiling faces and nimble fingers, one somehow instinctively feels the system of work adopted must have a wonderful influence for they are far removed from Midland and Northern types of factory "hands" as can be imagined.' [9]

And it was not only the girls that took the reporter's fancy for on his tour of the factory he remarked on the men:

'that judging from their general physique there must be something decidedly invigorating in their work for a finer set of men it would be difficult to find.' [10]

The reporter's visit was concluded by noting that:

'In management there is an enormous amount of vigour and business capability that augurs well for future prosperity.'

In that observation the reporter was certainly correct.

The third large firm of the area was Robinson's, a printing and stationery firm based at the top of Redcliffe Street, just a stone's throw from Bristol Bridge. The firm was founded on May 1st, 1844, a significant date that was also marked by the opening of the Bristol and Exeter Railway.

Robinson's most important products were stationery and paper bags. The introduction of the penny post in 1840 had done much to encourage sales of envelopes and stationery. Robinson's *Ancient Vellum* boasted that it 'contained none of the colouring matter so common and objectionable in cheap writing paper.'[12] With regard to paper bags it may come as a surprise to find that they were a novelty in the 1840s. Until Robinson's rectified the matter, paper bags were rarely used; grocers would merely place loose produce on a sheet of wrapping paper and fold the edges. A grocer might occasionally make a few bags in his spare time but few bothered for there was really little or no money to be made in packaging. Or so it was thought. Elisha Robinson, however, saw the potential for manufactured paper bags and with clever marketing and hard sales work he soon generated a need for them.

In 1846 Robinson's moved to 2 Redcliffe Street and in the following years took over many of the adjacent properties. With the widening of Redcliffe Street between 1875 and 1877 the opportunity was taken to build, on the same site, smart new premises to the design of William Bruce Gingell, the architect also responsible for the Bristol General Hospital. Like the rest of Victoria Street the building was in a robust style, built largely of brick with a corner tower topped by a cupola. It remained a landmark on the Bristol horizon for nearly 90 years.

Robinson's, like Wills, were not afraid to be technologically innovative. A machine was devised that produced 100-200 bags a minute, the factory producing, in all, one and three quarter million bags a week in 1883. The more expensive bags, however, were still made by hand. 'The process,' wrote the author of *Bristol at Work*, 'must be witnessed with a great amount of pleasure owing to the marvellous dexterity of the women.'[13] The women also worked with some of the machinery such as the ingenious envelope making machines. Printing, however, was the men's domain – Robinson's being involved in both letterpress and the finer art of lithography. Every year the firm would buy paintings, usually more sentimental or moralising than artistic, from the Royal Academy. The staff of ten artists would then assiduously translate them into lithographs to be used for Robinson's famous calendars and advertisements. Sometimes the lithographic plates, made from blocks of stone, could take up to seven weeks to prepare and in the more elaborate prints twelve such plates would be used.

It is recounted that at Christmas-time Elisha Robinson, in agreeably Dickensian manner would 'walk round the warehouse greeting all those he could, seeing that those who lived at a distance were in time to catch their trains and often giving Christmas boxes.'[14] Indeed Elisha Robinson was quite a character – not only was he an astute and innovative businessman, he was also at times a man of few words. Whilst on a business trip, on being told that there was a fire in his warehouse he merely telegraphed the company 'Put it out. Robinson.' [15]

Robinson's suffered two serious fires at its Redcliffe Street factory. The first, on April 1st, 1903, necessitated the rebuilding of a large part of the premises including the famous corner tower; the second was started by bombs on the night of November 24th, 1940 during one of the most intense air-raids experienced by Bristol during the Second World War.

What the writers from the *Practical Magazine* and *The Bristol Times and Mercury* omitted to mention in their glowing tales of industrial enterprise was just how hard the work was on the shop or factory floor. By today's standards the hours were long and exhausting. In the early 1870s the day at Robinson's commenced at 6.00am and continued until 7.00pm. Until 1857 it had been a six day working week, but from that date onwards a half day off on Saturday was also allowed. There were no other days off, no summer holidays, except for public holidays. Even so, not all employers were ruthless exploiters. Smothering paternalism largely kept the labour movement at bay, though when employers did overstep the mark the unions were quick to get involved. A dispute arose in 1892 at Sanders chocolate factory in Redcliffe Street when the women workers, who were already doing a long day, were expected to work another hour until 7.00pm. The women quickly enlisted the aid of the Gas Workers Union who helped bring about a suspension of the extension of hours. The problem did not end there though, for any of Sanders women who joined the union were dismissed from their jobs. The whole affair culminated in what came to be known as the Black Friday March. [16]

So far we have looked at stories of industrial success, but as always there is another side to the coin. Although the railways were of benefit to the majority they did not help everybody. In the older Southern Parishes some of the smaller traditional industries were being elbowed out, while many of the retailers suffered from the loss of the Welsh trade. Until the coming of the railways Bristol's trade hinterland had spread over the River Severn to South Wales; with the railway's penetration into that area this trade was lost.

But these setbacks were minor compared with the failure of Finzel's. 1879 was a year of industrial slump nationally – this, combined with a series of other factors, had a calamitous effect on the firm's trading position. Finzel's profits were not high, and by the end of the decade they had deteriorated even further. Over-investment in new property and warehouses had already weakened the company; this, together with fierce product competition from Liverpool, where charges for sugar importation were half those at Bristol, and a committed policy of free trade by Disraeli's government had further contributed to the firm's downfall. Despite several rescue attempts by local businessmen the refinery was finally and disastrously closed in 1881.

With Finzel's closed, the once flourishing sugar trade of Bristol disappeared. Alongside a direct workforce of 800 there were many other related workers – coopers, draymen, warehousemen who were also laid off. Perhaps a thousand jobs were lost in all. Although other companies were thriving, such a large number could not directly be assimilated into their workforces. It hit the Southern Parishes hard; many houses, crowded a few years previously, became untenanted, large warehouses were left idle and property generally depreciated in value. 'It is difficult to imagine' wrote the *Times and Mercury* 'the poverty and scale of dire misery that followed.' [17]

Other companies did continue to prosper. Elisha Robinson, on completion of a new building at 1 Redcliffe Street, announced 'Gentlemen, I have the finest printing factory in the West of England and neither I or those who come after me will ever want to enlarge it.'[18] How wrong he was. For just eleven years later Robinson were building further premises in less crowded Bedminster for the lithographic and colour printing department.

Likewise Wills, whose production rocketed from six and a half million cigarettes in 1884 to nearly 14 million in 1886, also looked southwards to Bedminster where they built their new factory, a commanding redbrick monolith, part of which still dominates East Street today. Of Wills' many brand names, Woodbines which sold at five a penny in paper packets and Three Castles were the most famous. The name Three Castles came from Thackeray's novel *'The Virginian'*: 'There's no sweeter tobacco comes from Virginia, and no better brand than Three Castles.'

In Redcliffe Street, in Bedminster and further afield both Robinson's and Wills continued to thrive.

Notes

1. Practical Magazine, *'Crystalised Sugar Messrs Finzel's Sugar Refinery* (Bristol, 1873) p.166
2. G. Meason, *The Official Illustrated Guide to the Great Western Railway* (1860) p.819
3. *Bristol Times*, September 28th, 1872
4. *Practical Magazine*, op cit, p.163
5. ibid, p.163
6. ibid, p.163
7. Bristol Times and Mirror *'Work in Bristol'* (1883) p.81-82
8. R. Till, *Wills of Bristol*, p.41
9. Bristol Times and Mirror *'Work in Bristol'* (1883) p.84
10. ibid, p.83
11. ibid, p.89
12. ibid, p.64
13. ibid, p.64
14. B. Darwin, *Robinsons of Bristol 1844-1944* (Bristol, 1945) p.23
15. ibid, p.21
16. E. Malos, *Bristol's Other History*, *'Bristol Women in Action 1859-1919.'* (1983) p.120
17. Bristol Times and Mercury *'Homes of the Bristol Poor.'* (1884) p.60
18. B. Darwin, op cit, p.22

Other Sources

B. Atkinson, *Trade Unions in Bristol* (1982)
R. A. Buchanan, *The Industrial Archaeology of Bristol* (1967)

EIGHT

FLICKERING INTO DARKNESS

With the introduction of both tramways and electricity, Bristol appeared to be heading purposefully towards the twentieth century. Horse-drawn trams were first introduced into the city in 1875, while another novelty soon to be found on the streets was electric lighting. Initial trials of electric street lighting in 1881 had proved uneconomic. But after pressure from several companies wishing to become involved, the Corporation, hoping to avoid any private monopoly, decided to go ahead with its own supplies. Various experiments were carried out; amongst several schemes one gentleman suggested the idea of harnessing the power that he believed could be generated by the ebb and flow of the Avon.

Eventually Bristol's first electricity generating station was opened in 1893 on Temple Back. Once a supply was established the City Council jealously guarded its monopoly of the production of electricity. When the Bristol Tramways and Carriage Company started to run electrically driven trams, the power had to be generated from a base just beyond the city boundaries at Beaconsfield Road, St George. The electrification of the trams brought improvements in service – they held more passengers, they travelled about half as fast again as the old horse-drawn trams, and they were cheaper - with the result that it became vital that a generating station was established in a more central position.[1]

After a long battle the Bristol Tramways Company won through and built an impressive new power station at the Counterslip on land previously occupied by Finzel's Sugar Refinery. Tactlessly, it was directly across the road from the unprepossessing Temple Back generating station which it swaggeringly dominated. Today, apart from the absence of the two enormous 180 feet chimneys at Temple Back, both buildings remain from the outside substantially the same.

Unfortunately the introduction of the electric light was unable to stop the community of Redcliffe, Temple and St Thomas flickering into darkness. A Board of Trade enquiry in 1908 into working class rents, housing and retail prices found the living conditions in the parish of Redcliffe to be still in the slum category. But in the Edwardian era working class poverty seemed to be no longer a matter of immediate concern. That the middle classes were content to disclaim any responsibility for them is exemplified by a series entitled 'Curious Living Places' published by the *Bristol Evening News* in 1908. Despite admitting that 'too often conditions which afford material for a picturesque drawing are

*After a long battle with the Corporation Bristol Tramway Company completed its impressive new
generating station in 1900 (background). It was across the road from the Temple Back Power
Station (foreground), which it swaggeringly dominated.*
(Photo M. Manson)

the very reverse of attractive when invested with the squalor of slum life,' the tone of the *Evening News'* articles was one of condescension.

'Looking down an alleyway one may detect with surprise a public lamp...and entering find a minute square surrounded by small houses or rows of little dwellings facing a narrow court. From one court there may in certain cases be passages leading to others...'

'How many thousands who hurry through Redcliffe Street have any idea what is implied by Warry's Court or Golden Lion Passage: Warry's Court...is entered by a passage above which the Redcliffe Street frontage extends. The passage is narrow but leads to a wider one open to the sky. In this space have been built in a line four pairs of small dwellings with tiny yards between the pairs. The opposite side of the court is bounded by a wall, on the other side of which is a timber yard, so for airspace the inhabitants are better off than others. Golden Lion Passage is so curious that a visitor wonders how it came into being. It might be accounted for if it be supposed that some former Bristolian owning a home in Redcliffe Street decided to pack a number of residences into his back garden. It is another case of utilising every inch of the ground...' [2]

It is at the beginning of the twentieth century that the story of our parishes falters. The community was already dying. The introduction of the railways had started this decline, as from that time onward the large scale industries began to stifle the smaller entrepreneurs who had given the community its life for so long. One of the final blows came with the widening of the notorious Redcliffe and Temple Streets. The personal businesses with their family accommodation above were destroyed only to be replaced by large soulless warehouses and factories. The community of Redcliffe, Temple and St Thomas had grown rotten with old age; the houses had decayed as had the reputation of their inhabitants. Any respectable person lived in the fresher air of the new suburbs and commuted to work by tram or train. Given the circumstances the only remedy to the malaise was to sweep away the remaining residential premises and give the whole area over to industry. Redcliffe, Temple and St Thomas turned from a community teeming with life into an area populated by gaunt warehouses and faceless factories.

In the 1930s slum clearance meant moving many families from the Southern Parishes to new residential areas, like Knowle West. Children could play in the fields and parks near their homes instead of the streets, and go to newer schools. Yet for some it was an unnerving change. The streets of Knowle West were so quiet – there was no humming of factory noise. Many claimed that they had been banished 'to a strange, quiet, tree-less plateau on the outskirts of the city.'

On account of its out-of-fashion architecture Victoria Street was known as the 'ugliest street in Europe.' To many visitors to Bristol, arriving at Temple Meads station was a daunting introduction to the city. In 1933, J.B Priestley wrote that all he ever knew of Bristol was 'Temple Meads Station in the dark hours, Victoria Street and the deserted smoke room of the hotel there. The natural result was that I carried with me the vague impression that this was an unpleasant city...' [3]

The slow process of the area's decline was unintentionally hastened by Hitler. The Luftwaffe had earmarked the factories and warehouses for their special attention. On Sunday November 24th, 1940, in one of Bristol's worst air-raids of the Second World War, Redcliffe, Temple and St Thomas, along with much of the city centre, were severely blitzed. Not only were commercial and industrial buildings destroyed but also many of the areas' historic landmarks. Temple Church, which had withstood the ravages of six hundred years, was completely gutted, though the famous leaning tower still stood as a monument to the skill of its medieval builders. (Sappers, not familiar with its alarming tilt viewed the tower as unsafe and were only just stopped from demolishing it.) Nearby, Burton's Almshouses whose history was almost as long as the history of our area was gone forever. St Mary Redcliffe narrowly missed a similar fate; bombs fell on Redcliffe Hill demolishing the infants school and blasting pieces of tramline into the air. One length of track plunged into the graveyard where it still remains as a graphic reminder of those perilous days.

In between the air-raids life carried on as normally as possible. To ease traffic congestion between Redcliffe Street and Bristol Bridge a long-planned new bridge was built linking Redcliffe Back with Welsh Back.

By the end of the war what was left of the community of the Southern Parishes had also been blown apart. Following the devastation of the land between Bristol Bridge and Temple Meads Station there was much debate about what to do with the area. Amongst others, proposals were put forward by the Rotary Club of Bristol recommending that the area be turned into an enormous civic centre. Under the Rotarians' plan, Victoria Street was to be widened to 120 feet (almost double its present width) and the rest of the area was to be given over to all the civic facilities that Bristol needed. The plan noted that 'it would make an attractive vista to meet the eyes of those coming into Bristol from Temple Meads or the airport.' [4]

Even though no such large scale schemes went ahead, under the pressure of post-war development what little was left of the community slowly disintegrated. The original area – to the north of Portwall Lane – became uninhabited, given over entirely to commerce and industry. The few remaining residents were re-housed in tower blocks and flats that dwarf even St Mary Redcliffe. Development in the 1960s saw the introduction of dual carriageways ripping across the district; a busy ring road passes by Chatterton's doorstep while that historical industrial landmark, the shot-tower disappeared under tarmac. In a final insult the Corporation even decided to alter the name of Redcliffe by dropping the last 'e.' [5]

NEW LIFE

By the early 1970s the waterfronts along Redcliffe and Temple Back were dreary and decaying. Large bomb sites from thirty years before were still undeveloped while many of the warehouses stood empty and rat infested. The aromatic smell of the tawny weed no longer wafted down Redcliffe Street. Wills' main factory was at Hartcliffe; its renaissance style building, after years of neglect, was finally demolished in 1976.

The Southern Parishes formed part of what a planning report was to define as a ring of dereliction surrounding the commercial core of the city. Bristol had to face the fact that the docks were an eyesore and that their decline was finally complete and irreversible. It was small consolation that the City was not alone in this decline. With the containerisation of ships the ports of both of Bristol's long term rivals – London and Liverpool – had suffered a similar fate.

By this time the immediate and urgent demands of post-war development had been attended to and planners were able to stand back and take time to deliberate as to how they wanted their city to look in the future. The real debate started in 1969 when the City Council put forward a proposal to 'partially reclaim' half of the area covered by the docks. The term 'partially reclaim' was a euphemism for fill-in. There was a public outcry; thankfully, Bristol's golden goose was not to be slaughtered that easily. In 1971, Casson, Conder and Partners, an independent group of consultant planners, were commissioned to produce a redevelopment study. Although good in parts, the Casson study was hampered by the City Council's potentially catastrophic insistence that it included a motorway running east-west along the docks, bridging the floating harbour at St Augustine's Reach and also at Wapping Wharf. Today such a proposal seems unthinkable, but this was an era when the car was king and the needs of the motorist were seen to be paramount.

Happily, many of the suggestions put forward by the 1972 Docks Redevelopment Study were eventually abandoned. The consultant planners did establish, however, two concepts that were to be of more lasting value – first, that widespread access to the docks should be made available to the citizens for recreational use and second, that new housing should be encouraged in the area.

These novel ideas took a while to become accepted. In the end it was left to a few far-sighted individuals, who saw the recreational potential of the large city centre waterspace, to make the move. Once the Arnolfini had established itself at Bush House right in the heart of the dereliction, things started to happen.

In 1977 an overall plan, this time produced by the City Planning Department, superseded the 1972 report with more specific recommendations on recreation and housing. The 1977 plan was of marked contrast in its scale and tone to the hasty post-war developments. The balance was changing in favour of keeping and adapting existing buildings and redeveloping on a smaller scale.

Merchants Landing, on the west side of Bathurst Basin: one of the first and probably most successful new housing developments breathing new life into the area.
(Photo M. Manson)

The twentieth century dock pioneers were soon followed by others who began to see the pleasures of waterside workplaces. New life was pumped into the docks. It has happened slowly. Development, under the ever-watchful eye of pressure groups such as the Bristol Civic Society, has been in a piecemeal, even organic way.

In the 1980s the gaps by Bristol Bridge and along part of Redcliffe Back were filled by brickwork buildings echoing the elaborate and imposing Victorian architecture they replaced. The intricacies of the Victorian Byzantine architecture began to be reappraised; it was realised that Victoria Street in its totality was rather impressive. But unfortunately this appreciation of high Victoriana came too late. Only the sympathetically restored facades of numbers 2-22 Victoria Street are left to remind us of the street's former glory.

Opposite, at the angle of Redcliffe Street and Victoria Street, the memory of Robinson's is still very much in evidence. Bags are no longer made there, though the company, in the form of DRG, built in 1964 Bristol's first tall office block – a stark 16 storeys and 250 feet high – as their administrative headquarters.

The DRG building overshadows another controversial development at the brewery in Bath Street. Courage's brewery was the last working industry left in central Bristol. Over the years, with Bath Street blocked off from public use and encompassed within the brewery site, the existence of a fine Georgian terrace built by Thomas Paty in the 1790s had been largely forgotten. Despite informed opposition, this made it easy in 1986 for Courage's to demolish half the row to make way for a lorry park. Yet this was a short-sighted plan – having a distribution depot in the middle of the city made little sense. Sixteen years on, Courage's have now abandoned the site – the Paty houses were thus needlessly destroyed. At the time of writing it seems that the site of the brewery will be turned over to offices and housing, bringing to an end a 200 year-old tradition of local brewing.

So industry has left; there are no sulphurous or other smells, no 24-hour clatter. Employment is mainly in the commercial sector; in the age of the computer and e-mail Bristol has proved popular with companies relocating from London. The waterfront has also become, for the first time in many, many years, an attractive place to live. The first and probably most successful of the housing to be built in this area is along the western side of Bathurst Basin. Since the Second World War, when the lock connecting to The Cut was filled-in to minimise the chances of bomb damage to the Float, the Basin had become something of a backwater, apart from use by Holms Sand and Gravel Company. The new development incorporated long-derelict Georgian housing and a splendid Bristol Byzantine seed mill. The renamed Merchants Landing waterfront development is impressive – only one thing rankles, and that is the change of name itself and the renaming of local inn, the Bathurst Tavern to The Louisiana. Street and place names are important and to change them for purely marketing reasons is historical vandalism.

At Merchants Landing the large, architecturally bland Turner Edwards Warehouse was demolished to make way for housing. Across the water at Buchanan's Wharf the two listed, eight-storey red brick mills were kept and converted in the mid 1980s into offices

The pleasures of waterside workplaces. Warehouses and bomb-sites by Bristol Bridge
were replaced in the 1980s by offices. After many centuries industry has largely
abandoned the parishes of Redcliffe, Temple and St Thomas.
(Photo M. Manson)

on the ground floor and flats above. Next door, the W.V Gough's WCA warehouse (built 1896) with its three distinctive overhanging hoist canopies was converted in 1997 into social housing.

Some of this new housing has been more successful than others in fostering a vibrant community. However attractive and well designed the waterfront accommodation is, some developments appear to lack the magic gel that enables people to live together as a community – rather than in their own pockets of isolation. And one block away from the waterfront it's the same old story. 'To arrive at Temple Meads and set out to walk into the city is a most dispiriting experience…It is one of the most depressing half-mile walks you can take in this country.' [6]

The curse of traffic congestion continues. Today, even bigger roads rip through the area. Road 'improvements' at the end of the twentieth Century have made little impact on the problem.[7] Between 1989 and 1991 abortive plans for a light railway system to alleviate congestion were developed by a private company Advanced Transport for Avon (ATA). The scheme foundered, however, due to uncertainty about its funding. At the time of writing a proposal for a tram system is rumbling over the horizon.

Throughout the Southern Parishes' long history we have seen how the infringement of local rights can lead to resentment, protest and sometimes violence. It comes as no surprise therefore that in 1988 local sensibilities were upset by the imposition by Margaret Thatcher's government of an Urban Development Corporation (UDC). The remit of the UDC was to develop derelict and disused land and vacant buildings in the east-central area of Bristol. It was a slap in the face for local democracy. Bristol City Council did not welcome this initiative. The council objected to their loss of planning and development powers and stated that many of the proposals put forward by the UDC were already in hand.[8]

Apart from further road building the most obvious legacy of the UDC is new offices, built on the old Temple Meads goods yard reminiscent, in scale and looks, of those soul-destroying buildings so beloved by iron-curtain dictators.

At the time of writing a draft framework, put forward by a private developer, for mixed-use development in Redcliff (sic) Village in the North Redcliffe area is on the drawing board. The emphasis of this new plan is 'Community focus' – something that has been all too evidently missing in the developments of the last half of the twentieth century.

In the 1988 edition of this book it was written that 'Perhaps, for the last hundred years the Southern Parishes have been not dead, but merely slumbering.' Twelve years later it is clear that although the land of the ancient Southern Parishes now forms part of Bristol's commercial heartland, and that residents are returning, hopes for a revived, cohesive community have, as yet, to be fully achieved.

Notes

1. P. G. Lamb, *Electricity in Bristol* (Bristol, 1981) p.15
2. G. F. Stone, *Bristol As It Was and Is* (Bristol, 1909) p.258-260
3. J. B. Priestley, *English Journey* (Penguin, 1977) p.29
4. *The Builder,* December 21st, 1945, p.500
5. City and County of Bristol, *Housing Nomenclature in Bristol* (1969) p.45
6. Bristol City Council, *Proposed Bristol Urban Development Corporation* (leaflet, no date or reference number, certainly 1998)
7. Bristol Evening Post 13 October 1988
8. The author laments the loss of the only piece of traffic engineering that was both practical and fun – the Temple Way temporary flyover – which was in use for over 25 years!

Selected Reading

Casson, Conder and Partners – *Redevelopment Study* (1972)
City Docks Joint Study Team, *Bristol City Docks Local Plan* (1977)
A. Gomme, M. Jenner, B. Little, *Bristol: An architectural history* (London, 1979)
G.Priest & P.Cobb, *The Fight for Bristol* (Redcliffe Press, 1980)
J. Lord & J. Southam, *The Floating Harbour* (Redcliffe Press, 1983)
T. Aldous, *Changing Bristol* (1979)
T. Aldous, *Bristol's Twentieth Century Buildings* (Redcliffe Press, 2000)
Reece Winstone's unique series of *As it Was* books contain an unrivalled photographic record of the city

INDEX

Temple Meads Market, 31, 112
Temple Meads Station, 97, 118, 127, 128, 133
Temple Street, 25, 56
– attack on meeting house, 62
– birth of E. Colston, 50
– mudslinging (1831), 94
– school, 48, 50
– widening, 116, 127
Tetbury, 19
Thatcher, Margaret, 133
Thomas Street, 24, 31, 39, 56, 64, 75
Tippet, Edward, 45
Tobacco, 120-121
Totterdown, 64
Tower of London, 43, 46
Transport
– by river, 62
– by road, 113
– tramways, 125
Treen Mills, 32, 34, 69, 86
Turner Edwards Warehouse, 131
Turnpikes, 62-64
Turnpike Act (1749), 64

Urban Development Corporation (U.D.C), 133

Vagrants, 32
Van Tromp, Admiral, 43
Venables, General, 43
Vermin Farm, 112
Vickris, Robert, 61
Victoria, Queen, 111
Victoria Street, 115, 116, 122, 127, 128

WCA Warehouse, 133
Walpole, Horace, 53, 72
Water, 69, 109
Watts, the plumber, 81-82
Weare, William, 113
Weavers, 16, 17
Wells, 44
West Indies, 48
Westbury-on-Trym, 36
Wetherall, Sir Charles, 93-95, 97
Wilberforce, William, 104
William III, King, 46
Wills WD & HO, 113, 118, 120-122, 129
Windsor Terrace, Clifton, 82

Woollen cloth
– decline of industry, 26-29
– manufacture, 17
Worcester, porcelain, 60
Worcester, William of, 24
Wotton-Under-Edge, 20

ALSO BY MICHAEL MANSON:

'RIOT!'

The BRISTOL BRIDGE MASSACRE *of* 1793.

ISBN 0-9532082-0-6
Softback, 108 pages, including 14 illustrations, price £6.95

'Riot!' illuminates a darker moment in Bristol's history. Set against a backdrop of massive social and political change 'Riot!' vividly recreates the dreadful sequence of events that led to the Bristol Bridge Massacre.

Compellingly written and meticulously researched 'Riot!' chronicles the events in Bristol during the pivotal year of 1793.

'Excellent.' *Bristol Evening Post*

'A well written and useful addition to the local history bookshelf.' *Bristol Civic Society Newsletter.*

'If local history isn't normally your thing, make an exception for this one.' *Venue*

'I have just finished reading 'Riot!' and enjoyed it immensely. It is excellent. It is graphically written and very clear. The background is well painted in, and the drama and the folly of the Corporation are beautifully drawn.' *Sir Ian Gilmour, author of 'Riots, Risings and Revolution'.*

Available through bookshops or directly from Past & Present Press for £6.95 (includes postage and packing).

past & present press   Past and Present Press, 92 Sefton Park Road, Bristol BS7 9AL
Tel: (0117) 924 9332 e-mail: pastandpresent@blueyonder.co.uk